THE PHILOSOPHY OF SHAKESPEARE

By the same author

TALKS ON PHILOSOPHY
THREE CHINESE THINKERS

THE PHILOSOPHY
OF SHAKESPEARE

by

K. J. SPALDING

Fellow of Brasenose College, Oxford

PHILOSOPHICAL LIBRARY
NEW YORK

Published 1953 by
Philosophical Library, Inc., 15 East 40th Street, New York, N.Y.

Copyright in Great Britain 1953 by George Ronald

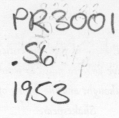

PRINTED IN GREAT BRITAIN
FOR PHILOSOPHICAL LIBRARY INC., BY
EBENEZER BAYLIS AND SON, LTD., THE
TRINITY PRESS, WORCESTER, AND LONDON

Dedicated
without permission
to all those writers and critics
who have done so much to interpret
the thought and the drama of
Shakespeare

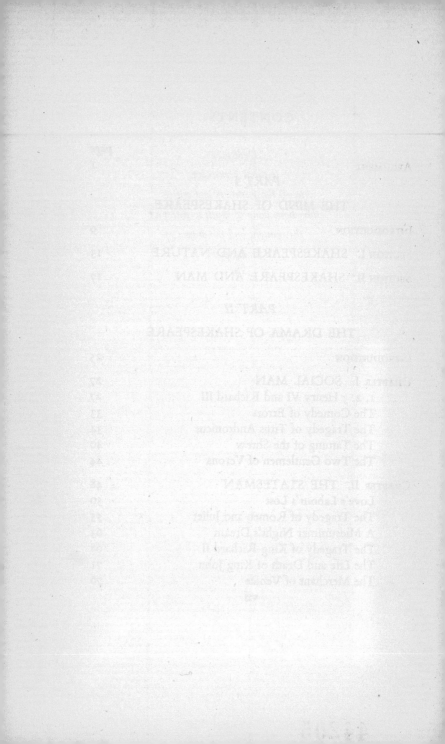

CONTENTS

vii

CONTENTS

ARGUMENT

SHAKESPEARE's plays seem, at first sight, to reveal a mind remarkable rather for its imagination than for its logic: a mind that, replete with the most contradictory experiences, gives equally generous expression to all of them and like the wind blows indifferently on his hearers from all points of the compass. The gentle breeze of *A Midsummer Night's Dream* readily follows the tempest of *Romeo and Juliet*; and in a single play like *Richard II* Shakespeare's readers may be left wondering whether to believe with his Duke of Milan that

> Much is the force of heaven-bred poesy,

or to follow, rather, his more sceptical Duke of Athens in finding the "poet" appropriately consorting with "the lunatic" and "the lover".

Wayward in some degree as Shakespeare's mind may thus appear to be, yet it seems somewhat unlikely that it could be one as rich as it is without being richer. The heavenly bodies are of an endless variety; yet their variety would be no better than an irrational chaos were it not to be ordered by the mathematical logic of the astronomer and astrophysicist. As full of ideas as the sky is of bodies the mind of Shakespeare must be similarly a mere chaos were no philosophical logic respecting the nature of things to give it some rational order and meaning. Shakespeare was no professional philosopher like Aristotle. Yet like Aristotle he may well have been concerned to reveal to men the real nature of 'man', or, with the failure in them of that nature, to offer them some remedy which, like that of Jacques in *As You Like It*, might

I   A*

Cleanse the foul body of the infected world.

A study of Shakespeare's earlier dramas seems to reveal such a remedial purpose as may thus be plausibly expected of them. After considering the chaos of man's actual world (Chap. I), like the scientist confronted by the empirical chaos of Nature he proceeds, it seems, to look for some rational remedy for its irrationalities (Chap. II). Presenting in different plays different maladies of men and of the State, he likewise presents in them some physician with the task of alleviating or healing them. The 'physician' may be able but unlucky—like Friar Laurence in *Romeo and Juliet*; unable and a failure, like Richard II; able but severe, like Henry IV; able and invigorating, like Henry V. And Shakespeare might sometimes delight his audience by introducing a lady doctor to his afflicted patients; as Portia in *The Merchant of Venice*; or Rosalind in *As You Like It*. As he proceeds Shakespeare seems, however, to have become less hopeful of the efficacy of the human will in healing human disorders. In *Hamlet* he presents an Idealist unable with the vigour of a Hercules to cleanse a world as foul for his thought as the stable of Augeas. In *Troilus and Cressida*, again, sick men are presented irrationally lording it over their protesting physicians. Yet "all's well that ends well". In Helena Shakespeare depicts a girl as competent to heal the spirit of a Count as the body of a King; and in Duke Vincentio of Vienna one ready at last truly to "cleanse the foul body of the infected world" through a remedial love of man for man deriving from Heaven's own Mercy towards Its creatures.

Studied thus for their remedial function, men, however, may be studied further for their own sake (Chap. III). A being "how infinite in faculty! in apprehension how like a god!", man is a cosmic creature as well as a political animal; a member

2

of the universe as well as of a society. Be man as perfect however as he may be, he may fail to be completely 'man', for—

> no perfection is so absolute
> That some impurity doth not pollute.

However imperfect, the "paragon of animals" may, on the
other hand, attain perfection, and like the Prodigal Son come
in time "to himself". In *Othello* and *Macbeth* Shakespeare
appears to be studying the fall of a man through jealousy or
through ambition: in *King Lear* the rise, rather, of a man
through the discipline of suffering; and in *Antony and Cleopatra*
and *Coriolanus*, the fall of a man and the rise of a woman.

In a variety of his plays Shakespeare shows himself aware of
a divinity in the world, that "shapes our ends, rough-hew
them how we will". The work of his 'physicians' was itself
subject to Its over-ruling Providence. For Friar Laurence It
was—

> A greater power than we can contradict;

for Henry V it was the "arm" to which alone must be ascribed
the work of princes. This Power is one, however, that
gives rise to perplexities more troublesome to a philosopher
than to other men. To Its necessary perfection the tragic evil
of man's world can be ascribed by no likely venture of logic.
Yet as little can it be ascribed to men who, born with some
"vicious mole of nature" cannot be considered "guilty" of the
evils it determines in them (*Hamlet*, 1, 4, 24). A serpent is
born to sting in its own time; an Othello, as surely, it may
be, to be jealous in his. Uncaused by Heaven's Providence or
by human choice, evil, it seems, can only be conceived to
issue from the Causeless Chance that men name Fate or
Fortune; and for a while Shakespeare seems to have studied
the play of Fate on the lives of an Othello, a Macbeth, an

3

Antony, a Coriolanus. A world thus fated to fall might awake in his mind for a time the pangs of a Timon. Yet, like the scientist confronted by the Chance of Nature, Shakespeare's more rational spirit presently endeavoured rather to resolve his perplexities than to remain their victim; and in his latest dramas he conceived of Fate, no longer as the root in man of a "particular fault" that, like a mole of nature, blasted his beauty, but rather as a Heavenly Cause that, through Its influence upon the wills of human beings, destined them to a repentance consistent with Heaven's acceptance of them (Chap. IV). Through such instruments of Heaven as Marina, Imogen, Hermione, erring men might inevitably come in time "to themselves", and, with Heaven's own fate to help them, sing at last—

> The fingers of the powers above do tune
> The harmony of this peace.

For the logic of Shakespeare there remained however in the world a mystery still to be fathomed. Heaven might doom the evil of the world, but why It should ever have admitted it into the world would seem to be one "of those mysteries that heaven will not have earth to know". To this last question Shakespeare addressed himself (Chap. V), and in *The Tempest* studied the mysterious word of a god to an afflicted sinner:

> Whom best I love, I cross; to make my gift,
> The more delay'd, delighted. (*Cym.*, 5. 4.)

It is the task of the Heaven-led Prospero to pour crosses on men

> lest too light winning
> Make the prize light.

Heaven's kindness may send Its crosses on wandering men

4

like the Father on the Prodigal Son: thereby to win them gifts not offered to unerring men.

Bring forth quickly the best robe, and put it on him. . . . For this my son was dead, and is alive again: he was lost, and is found.

Shakespeare had experienced this mysterious "benefit of ill" in his own life, and with its explanation of the purpose of man's irrational evil his logic reaped its harvest:

O benefit of ill! now I find true
That better is by evil still made better;
And ruin'd love, when it is built anew,
Grows fairer than at first, more strong, far greater.
So I return rebuked to my content,
And gain by ill thrice more than I have spent.
(*Son.* 119)

PART I

THE MIND OF SHAKESPEARE

INTRODUCTION

SHAKESPEARE may seem at first sight to have few of the characteristics of the philosopher. Yet poets and artists may be philosophers—philosophers more sensitive at times to the truth of things than those who endeavour to express it by reason and argument. There are however two distinct types of philosopher: the empirical and the idealist. The empirical philosopher attempts to describe the world as he finds it. The idealist, rather, is predisposed to find a beauty in it pleasing to his reason; to listen for a tune in it. He is an expectant lover of the universe; a man that looks to be "saluted and surrounded with innumerable joys" (Traherne, *Centuries of Meditations*, III, 2).

Like the empiricist the idealist may enjoy the world peculiar to him in early childhood. "Heaven", says Wordsworth, "lies about us in our infancy"; and it was the experience of Traherne to enjoy "sweet and curious apprehensions of the world" when he was a child. "I seemed as one brought into the Estate of Innocence. All things were spotless and pure and glorious. . . . I knew not that there were any sins, or complaints or laws. I dreamed not of poverties, contentions or vices. . . . In the absence of these I was entertained like an Angel with the works of God in their splendour and glory" (III, 2).

Minds of this kind instinctively seek out all things that they may be loved. "They are unattainable by book" (III, 1) and men's experience itself must be their tutor. They have not far to go to find their heart's content. "The green trees when I first saw them . . . transported and ravished me, their sweetness and unusual beauty made my heart to leap . . . they were such strange and wonderful things. The Men! O what venerable and reverend creatures did the aged seem! . . . And young men glittering and sparkling Angels, and maids strange seraphic pieces of life and beauty! . . . Eternity was manifest in the light of the Day, and something infinite behind everything appeared: which talked with my expectation and moved my desire" (III. 3). United with the world as the lover with his mistress Spirits of this kind may say at last: "You never enjoy the world aright, till the Sea itself floweth in your veins, till you are clothed with the heavens, and crowned with the stars; and perceive yourself to be the sole heir of the whole world, and more than so, because men are in it who are every one sole heirs as well as you. Till you can sing and rejoice and delight in God, as misers do in gold, and Kings in sceptres, you never enjoy the world." (I. 29)

The enjoyment however of such Spirits is not without its vicissitudes. If Heaven lies about them in their infancy, yet

> Shades of the prison-house begin to close
> Upon the growing Boy . . . ;
> The Youth, who daily farther from the east
> Must travel, still is Nature's priest,
> And by the vision splendid
> Is on his way attended;
> At length the Man perceives it die away,
> And fade into the light of common day.

"With much ado", Traherne in turn records, "I was corrupted and made to learn the dirty devices of this world: which now", his better self could claim, "I unlearn, and become, as it were, a little child again." Tragic as these "Apostasies" are to those who suffer them, yet those things they once knew "by intuition" they learn at last to "collect again by the highest reason" (III. 2).

An experience of this peculiar kind may not have been unknown to Shakespeare. In his maturity he recalled, it seems,
a lost "Estate of Innocence" depicted by him in two cherubs
who "knew not that there were any sins":

> We were as twinn'd lambs that did frisk i' the sun,
> And bleat the one at the other: what we changed
> Was innocence for innocence; we knew not
> The doctrine of ill-doing, nor dream'd
> That any did.   (*The Winter's Tale*, 1. 2. 67)

Love's hunger for the knowledge that feeds it seems to be
recalled in Shakespeare's thought of the young Posthumus
(*Cymbeline*, 1. 1. 43). Put "to all the learnings that his time
could make him the receiver of", the youth took them—

> As we do air, fast as 'twas minister'd,
> And in's spring became a harvest.

It may have been his thirst for knowledge that led Shakespeare
in his youth to seek his fortunes "farther than at home"
(*Taming of Shrew*, 1. 2. 50). He might find in London, like
Socrates in Athens, a place more likely to satisfy his cravings
than one "where small experience grows". (cf. *Two Gent.*,
1. 3. 4–23.)

Shakespeare was not however to escape the "Apostasy"
which troubles other natures of this kind. A lady well-nigh
sealed his eyes for a while to every beauty of the world but
her own. His lust for her was one—

> Past reason hunted; and no sooner had
> Past reason hated.   (*Son.* 129)

She was a lure, he knew, that made him "give the lie to
his true sight" (*Son.* 150); a girl who, in betraying him,
betrayed—

My nobler part to my gross body's treason.

(*Son.* 151)

Yet Shakespeare's 'Apostasy' endured in him as little as it endured in Traherne. His tripping mistress's dark eyes were not to be forgotten by him. But the madness of her magic waned in time in him like a dream. In his *Venus and Adonis* Shakespeare appears to be recording for himself and others an example of feminine lust (ll. 553–564) at war with love's true graces (ll. 799–810): in his *Rape of Lucrece*, a warning of the fate to which love's "doting" may lead undisciplined tempers (ll. 498–504, 1849–1855). Like the Prodigal Son Shakespeare presently "came to himself". The things he once knew in his "estate of innocence" he gradually collected again "by the highest reason"; and, in the "fountain light of all our day", came to see more distinctly perhaps than before his 'Apostasy' —together with "the sweetness and unusual beauty" of natural things—the venerable "Men" again; and "young men glittering and sparkling Angels, and maids strange seraphic pieces of life and beauty".

SHAKESPEARE AND NATURE

EMPIRICAL thought studies the objects of Nature in their relation to the body; idealistic, rather, in their relation to the mind. As convinced as the Empiricist of the worth of the body, the Idealist yet rates the mind above it. For what, the Idealist asks, is a man—

> If his chief good and market of his time
> Be but to sleep and feed? a beast, no more.
> Sure, he that made us with such large discourse,
> Looking before and after, gave us not
> That capability and god-like reason
> To fust in us unused. (*Hamlet*, 4. 4. 33)

This reason in man presents for his enjoyment things more precious to him than riches. "This goodly frame, the earth; this most excellent canopy, the air; this brave o'erhanging firmament; this majestical roof fretted with golden fire" (*Ham.*, 2. 2. 310) are treasures of Nature which, surpassing the pleasures of animals, bring joy to men's awakened "reason".

> All places that the eye of heaven visits
> Are to a wise man ports and happy havens.
> (*Rich. II*, 1. 3. 275)

The earth for him is full of moving sights and sounds and odours. For Shakespeare its innumerable contents were as full of beauties as they were for Wordsworth. A Peter Bell might be more anxious for his food than for its flowers;

A primrose by a river's brim
A yellow primrose was to him,
And it was nothing more.

But to Shakespeare primroses were beauties to "sweeten" a "sad grave" (*Cym.*, 4. 2. 220). The least of animals stirred the poet's ready pleasure.

Poor harmless fly,
That, with his pretty buzzing melody,
Came here to make us merry;
(*Tit. An.*, 3. 2. 63)

and he could feel for a beetle in a manner that his wife perhaps could hardly approve of:

The poor beetle, that we tread upon,
In corporal sufferance finds a pang as great
As when a giant dies. (*M. for M.*, 3. 1. 79)

One thing surpasses another in beauty, and to Shakespeare the "paragon of animals" appeared the paragon of beauties. One girl may as much exceed another

in beauty as the first of May doth the last
of December (*Much Ado*, 1. 1. 176);

and in a loveliest of girls Shakespeare finally imagined "the most peerless piece of earth, I think, that e'er the sun shone bright on" (*W.T.*, 5. 1. 94). It was however Shakespeare's fortune to find an earlier beauty of this kind in a "lovely boy" of his acquaintance whose fair parts—

Want nothing that the thought of hearts can mend.
(*Son.* 69)

Yet, if beauty commonly triumphed in Nature, Nature at times might strangely defeat it.

14

> Diseased nature oftentimes breaks forth
> In strange eruptions. . . . (I *Hen. IV*, 3. 1. 27)

Storms as boundless as the tempests of Turner will sometimes "wash both heaven and hell" (*Pericles*, 3. 1. 2); and vainly in the "little world of man" will man endeavour to out-scorn "the to-and-fro-conflicting wind and rain" that "drench his steeples, drown the cocks" (*Lear*, 3. 1. 10; 3. 2. 3). Living things will prey on one another. Weeds smother lovelier things than themselves, and

> in the sweetest bud
> The eating canker dwells.
> (*Two Gent.*, 1. 1. 42).

The fairest thing alive is as subject as "the teeming earth" to Nature's "strange eruptions": as "burning fevers, agues pale and faint . . ."—

> And not the least of all these maladies
> But in one minute's fight brings beauty under.
> (*V. and A.*, l. 739)

Were beauty free from these alarms, a yet more cruel fate awaits it—

> For never-resting time leads summer on
> To hideous winter and confounds him there.
> (*Son.* 5)

"Mis-shapen Time", "eater of youth" (*Lucrece*, ll. 925–7), with every other thing devours the fairest. The "lovely boy" is not less subject to his "scythe" than things more meet for it. For him too

> Time that gave doth now his gift confound,
> (*Son.* 60)

and, feeding "on the rarities of nature's truth", irrevocably

> doth transfix the flourish set on youth,
> And delves the parallels in beauty's brow.
>
> (*Son.* 60)

Love looks and longs for beauty's immortality. But it can, as it searches, find it only as the loved one lives again in his own sons (*Son.* 1–16), or in the verses of a poet (*Son.* 17–25).

SHAKESPEARE AND MAN

"What a piece of work is a man! how noble in reason!
how infinite in faculty! in form and moving how
express and admirable! in action how like an angel!
in apprehension how like a god! the beauty of the
world! the paragon of animals!" (*Hamlet*, 2. 2. 315)

IF the beauty of a thing of Nature touched the heart of
Shakespeare, the beauty of a human mind touched it more
deeply. Mind knows itself and all things; bodies know neither
themselves nor other things. Man's "noble reason" presents
accordingly for his enjoyment things which, invisible though
they be to the eye, are more precious to him than "this goodly
frame, the earth".

"By seeing farther than the eye hath shown" (*Son*. 69),
Shakespeare perceived combining with the beauty of the body
the greater beauty of the mind. In some "estate of innocence"
he may artlessly have caught this double beauty with the
thrill of Prospero's young daughter:

> O, wonder!
> How many goodly creatures are there here!
> How beauteous mankind is! O brave new world,
> That has such people in't! (*Tempest*, 5. 1. 181)

Men and women of this kind act like magnets on one another.
"Seeming parted" they yet form, like Helena and Hermia, "an
union in partition" (*M.N.D.*, 3. 2. 209):

> Two distincts, division none,
> Number there in love was slain.
>> (*Phoenix and Turtle*, l. 27)

Thus one with one another men may say, like Celia of Rosalind, "Thou and I am one" (*As You Like It*, 1. 3. 99); and to them "I am I" (*R. III*, 5. 3. 183) is an inhuman unit.

Content with one another, and with Nature's beauties, such unspoiled minds prefer the simple to the artificial, and are more at home in country places than in polished cities.

> Are not these woods
> More free from peril than the envious court?
> Here feel we but the penalty of Adam,
> The seasons' difference. . . .
> And this our life exempt from public haunt
> Finds tongues in trees, books in the running brooks,
> Sermons in stones and good in every thing.
>> (*A.Y.L.*, 2, 1, 3)

Men who think no crime can need no law; nor letters, whose tongues are trees and books the running brooks; nor toil, who are content with Nature's own gifts to them. In their childlike Commonwealth the voyager would find—

> no name of magistrate;
> Letters should not be known; riches, poverty,
> And use of service, none . . .
> No occupations; all men idle, all;
> And women too, but innocent and pure.
>> (*Tempest*, 2. 1. 149)

Yet—

> the more fair and crystal is the sky,
> The uglier seem the clouds that in it fly.
>> (*R. II*, 1. 1. 41)

The beauty to be looked for in man is in him more miserably defeated than the beauty of the sensible world. Expelling 'nature' (*Tempest*, 5. 1. 76); himself 'himself' misusing (*R. III*, 4. 4. 376); man unnaturally tears himself from man; loses the love that "teaches him that thou and I am one"; and ceases to be 'himself'. Unloving; ungrateful; unforgiving; lustful, doting; jealous, envious and ambitious; wealth-desiring, luxurious and artificial; a betrayer of men, hypocritically parading the nature "expelled" by him:—with his unending evils man irrationally troubles the State and, with himself, throws his world into chaos. Lovely bodies may still trip through this world; but "beauty lives with kindness", it may seem now, only in a song (*Two Gent.*, 4. 2. 44). By mimicking their mirth Shakespeare could make rogues enchanting; and fools amusing by falling in with their folly. But as he gazed at the untempting lives of men and women around him he might have said with Traherne: "Verily, the prospect of their ugly errors is able to turn one's stomach; they are so hideous and deformed" (*C. of M.*, I. 33):—

> Tired with all these, for restful death I cry,
> As, to behold desert a beggar born,
> And needy nothing trimm'd in jollity,
> And purest faith unhappily forsworn,
> And gilded honour shamefully misplaced,
> And maiden virtue rudely strumpeted,
> And right perfection wrongfully disgraced,
> And strength by limping sway disabled,
> And art made tongue-tied by authority,
> And folly, doctor-like, controlling skill,
> And simple truth miscall'd simplicity,
> And captive good attending captain ill:
> > Tired with all these, from these would I be gone,
> > Save that, to die, I leave my love alone.
> > > (*Son.* 66)

Disillusioned with the world he had conceived to be fair, Shakespeare could live only through the one remaining Beauty that seemed still to fulfil his ideal (*Son.* 67)—only through his "lovely boy" whose "sum of good" now made for him his only "home of love" (*Son.* 109):

> all the world besides methinks are dead
>
> (*Son.* 112)

and

> nothing this wide universe I call,
> Save thou, my rose; in it thou art my all.
>
> (*Son.* 109)

Shakespeare's "angel" (*Son.* 144) became for a time as much his saviour as his gipsy mistress his destroyer. Yet "pretty looks" of hers were to prove the inconstancy even of Shakespeare's "unstained" Beauty (*Son.* 70).

> Me from myself thy cruel eye hath taken,
> And my next self thou harder hast engrossed.
>
> (*Son.* 133)

To the poet's anguish his "sweet boy" grew guilty of an "apostasy" as irrational as his own (*Son.* 147); and, "with base infection meeting", turned the sweetest thing in his world the "sourest" for him (*Son.* 94).

> The apprehension of the good—
> Gives but the greater feeling to the worse.
>
> (*R. II*, 1. 3. 300)

Eyes that see men only "in the light of common day" feel little as men's familiar vices throw their shadows on them. But to have lost the sight of men and women "glittering Angels" and "strange seraphic pieces of life and beauty" is, with their eclipse, to know light darkness and life death. Men

20

become, for such eyes, monstrous rather than human; in apprehension how like devils! things they must rather break from than cleave to: must reject rather than enjoy; must cease to love; must will to die.

> Common mother, thou, . . .
> Ensear thy fertile and conceptious womb,
> Let it no more bring out ingrateful man!
>
> > (*Timon*, 4. 3. 177)

Sick at heart Shakespeare could fall, as he watched the human scene, into despondencies and anguishes uncouth and strange to common men: in "this majestical roof fretted with golden fire" could see no more than a "foul congregation of vapours"; and, in the life of man, a baseless "dream", the better ended.

PART II

THE DRAMA OF SHAKESPEARE

INTRODUCTION

Why should the worm intrude the maiden bud? . . .
Or tyrant folly lurk in gentle breasts?
Or kings be breakers of their own behests?
     But no perfection is so absolute
     That some impurity doth not pollute.
                     (*Luc.*, l. 848)

Like Nature man presents a riddle to the mind. Reason looks for the perfection of either, but experience discovers imperfections in both. In this quarrel reason wins the final word. For the astronomer the seeming motions of the planets are not their real motions; and for the moral philosopher the seeming man is not the real man.

    Thou art not what thou seem'st; and if the same,
    Thou seem'st not what thou art, a god, a king.
                     (*Luc.*, l. 600)

As the scientist looks for a rational order in the seeming disorder of the natural world, so the moral philosopher looks for one in the seemingly disordered and chaotic life of man. To find this hidden reason in man's mortal world is his problem; though the further he delves into its actual disorders, the more difficult it may appear to him to discover it. A world to "turn a man's stomach" can only invite him to look for something pleasanter in it; and Shakespeare, it seems, was as anxious as Aristotle to discover a remedy for its irrationalities. Following the light that at any time came to him, he aimed at making known to himself and to others, with the evil

                                                               B

infections that fevered himself and all other men (*A.Y.L.*, 2. 7. 62–87), the medicine necessary to their recovery:

> give me leave
> To speak my mind, and I will through and through
> Cleanse the foul body of the infected world,
> If they will patiently receive my medicine.
>
> (*A.Y.L.*, 2. 7. 59)

If Shakespeare speaks sometimes as drily as a philosopher, he did not however set off for London to write philosophical treatises. His genius, in Ruskin's words, compelled him to express "the piece of true knowledge or sight which his share of sunshine and earth had permitted him to seize" in the more concrete and vivid form of the Drama. It was not without difficulty that the poet practised this art. As a player he might meet, like other artists, with the world's contempt or indifference; and "in disgrace with fortune and men's eyes" might "all alone beweep" his "outcast state" (*Son.* 29). Other difficulties harassed the mind of the poet. Philosophers may live conveniently among the stars; but Shakespeare was bound by the duty of providing for the family he had strangely deserted. An Aristotle has the privilege of writing what he thinks. But Shakespeare had need to consider at once his partners, his actors and the pleasure of his public. In pursuing his problem he might at times be forced to "gore" his own thought—to sell "cheap what is most dear" (*Son.* 110); and might find it impracticable to utter truths plain to himself but strange to the multitude, and not less strange, perhaps, to a Kempe or a Burbage.

CHAPTER I

SOCIAL MAN

IT may have been under direction that Shakespeare wrote his first dramatic compositions. In

1, 2, 3 HENRY VI AND RICHARD III

he seems to be studying the social nature of man as revealed in the political chronicles of Halle and Holinshed. The poet found little enough to comfort him in them. They are the record of an England that "hath long been mad" (*R. III*, 5. 5. 23); of a people that had been for generations in irrational conflict with itself. Man is by nature a 'political animal'; and Shakespeare could observe disorder in the State only with the eye with which he observed disorder in the individual. The more deeply the poet peered into this benighted England, the darker it may have looked to him. Here he saw men and women self-enclosed and self-esteeming; ambitious; proud; disloyal. Here were sovereigns "breakers of their own behests"; princes "truant in the law" that could confess like Suffolk: "I never yet could frame my will to it; and therefore frame the law unto my will" (1 *H. VI*, 2. 4. 7):—authors therefore of rank revolt in the land; and of rebels scarcely less ill-disciplined and savage than themselves (2 *H. VI*, 4. 7).

> Women are soft, mild, pitiful and flexible.
> (3 *H. VI*, 1. 4. 141)

Yet here to be "wonder'd at" is to be found a woman "stern, obdurate, flinty, rough, remorseless". In Queen Margaret

Shakespeare painted a "beauty"—a "nature's miracle"—whose "chief perfections"

> Would make a volume of enticing lines.
> (1 *H. VI*, 5. 3. 54; 5. 5. 14)

Yet the "stuff within" this lady failed to match her "outward" form. If to the doting Suffolk she appeared provided with "a humble lowliness of mind" (*Ib.*, 5. 5. 18), to other eyes she looked a creature "as opposite to every good, as the Antipodes are unto us": a creature imperious; savage; inhuman; "abominable"—a "tiger's heart, wrapped in a woman's hide" (3 *H. VI*, 1. 4. 137):

> *Marg.*　　　　　Where is your darling Rutland?
> Look, York, I stain'd this napkin with the blood
> That valiant Clifford, with his rapier's point,
> Made issue from the bosom of the boy;
> And if thine eyes can water for his death,
> I give thee this to dry thy cheeks withal . . .
> I prithee grieve, to make me merry, York . . .
> Stamp, rave, and fret, that I may sing and dance.
> Thou would'st be fee'd, I see, to make me sport:
> York cannot speak, unless he wear a crown.
> A crown for York! and, lords, bow low to him:
> Hold you his hands, whilst I do set it on.
> 　　　　　　　(*Putting a paper crown on his head*).
> 　　　　　　　(3 *H. VI*, 1. 4. 78)

But—

> 　　　　　Where is that devil's butcher,
> Hard-favour'd Richard?　(3 *H. VI*, 5. 5. 77)

In Marlowe-like lines Shakespeare offered his audience the sight of a monster yet more inhuman than Queen Margaret. In Richard the Third the outward form agreed with the inner man: the one was as unnatural as the other. Save only in his

28

ceaseless energy Richard was the total opposite of Shakespeare's ideal Man.   Arriving in the world with "his legs
forward"—

> The midwife wondered, and the women cried
> 'O, Jesus bless us, he is born with teeth!'
> And so I was; which plainly signified
> That I should snarl, and bite, and play the dog.
> Then, since the heavens have shap'd my body so,
> Let hell make crook'd my mind to answer it . . .
> And this word 'love', which greybeards call divine,
> Be resident in men like one another,
> And not in me; I am myself alone.
>
> (3 *H. VI*, 5. 6. 74)

"Richard loves Richard; that is, I am I" (*R. III*, 5. 3. 183).
A creature without the love that teaches man that "thou and
I am one"; an egoist self-parted from his partners; Richard
lives a stranger in the world—a solitary in a crowd. Thus dis-
natured he can see in men no more than servants of his
sovereign pleasures; the offered food, to take or to reject, of
his rich appetites.   Unresponsive as men must be to the dis-
closure of such purposes with them, he must needs "seem a
saint" when most he "plays the devil" (*R. III*, 1, 3, 338). He
must show himself to them the being he is not; and, pious-
looking, clothe his "naked villany, with old odd ends stolen
out of holy writ" (*R. III*, 1. 3. 337).

> Why, I can smile, and murder whiles I smile,
> And cry 'Content' to that which grieves my heart,
> And wet my cheeks with artificial tears . . .
> I can add colours to the chameleon,
> Change shapes with Proteus, for advantages,
> And set the murderous Machiavel to school.
> Can I do this and cannot get a crown?
>
> (3 *H. VI*, 3. 2. 182)

The crown his cleverness won for him proved however in the end a fatal one. As "opposite" as Margaret to "every good", Richard was doomed, in winning it, to lose himself. Not quit of "all remorse and nature", the murderous king was preyed on by a conscience with "a thousand several tongues".

> *Ghost* When I was mortal, my anointed body
> By thee was punched full of deadly holes:
> Think on the Tower and me: despair, and die!
>
> (*R. III*, 5. 3. 124)

Midnight dreams of his dead victims thronged, at the last, round Richard.

> *Richard* Have mercy, Jesu!—Soft! I did but dream.
> O coward conscience, how dost thou afflict me! ...
> Cold fearful drops stand on my trembling flesh ...
> All several sins, all used in each degree,
> Throng to the bar, crying all 'Guilty! guilty!'
> I shall despair. There is no creature loves me;
> And if I die, no soul will pity me:
> Nay, wherefore should they, since that I myself
> Find in myself no pity to myself?
> Methought the souls of all that I had murder'd
> Came to my tent, and every one did threat
> To-morrow's vengeance on the head of Richard.
>
> (*R. III*, 5. 3. 178)

In human affairs, however, good often mingles with evil as sunshine with shadows. In a simple child of history Shakespeare found glimmerings of man's unspoiled "estate of innocence". "Anointed king at nine months old" (3 *H. VI*, 3. 1. 76), in a world of confusion this child constantly maintained a nature tender; pitiful; unready to think evil (2 *H. VI*, 3. 1. 67–73).

> Fam'd for mildness, peace, and prayer,
> > (3 *H. VI*, 2. 1. 156)

he consistently endeavoured to temper the storms of his tempestuous people.

> *K. Hen. VI* I prithee, peace, good queen,
> > And whet not on these furious peers;
> > For blessed are the peacemakers on earth.
> > > (2 *H. VI*, 2. 1. 33)

A porer over books, the holy man could hardly appear an intelligent being to the industrious creatures of ambition around him.

> *Q. Marg.* His study is his tilt-yard, and his loves
> > Are brazen images of canonized saints.
> > > (2 *H. VI*, 1, 3, 57)

As simple in age as he was in childhood Henry remained "a pupil still" to the threats or the behests of princes better versed than himself in the wiles of the world:

> Here on this molehill will I sit me down,
> To whom God will, there be the victory!
> For Margaret my queen, and Clifford too,
> Have chid me from the battle; swearing both
> They prosper best of all when I am thence.
> > (3 *H. VI*, 2. 5. 14)

"Tired with all these", Henry looked at last for death

> if God's good will were so!—

or in a private life to "spend my latter days, to sin's rebuke, and my Creator's praise" (3 *H. VI*, 4. 6. 43).

> For what is in this world but grief and woe?
> O God! methinks it were a happy life,

> To be no better than a homely swain . . .
> Gives not the hawthorn-bush a sweeter shade
> To shepherds looking on their silly sheep,
> Than doth a rich embroider'd canopy
> To kings that fear their subjects' treachery?
>
> (3 *H. VI*, 2. 5. 20)

The tricks of a Court surpassed the natural bounds of Henry's innocent understanding. Unadapted to plumb the natures of the men around him, he was as incapable of forecasting their future behaviour (3 *H. VI*, 4. 8. 33–50) as of relieving their present necessities:

K. Hen. And as the dam runs lowing up and down,
  Looking the way her harmless young one went,
  And can do nought but wail her darling's loss,
  Even so myself bewails good Gloucester's case
  With sad unhelpful tears, and with dimm'd eyes
  Look after him, and cannot do him good.

> (2 *H. VI*, 3. 1. 214)

Yet, troubled as he was, there lived in this child-man a peace not known to Richard:

> My crown is in my heart, not on my head;
> Not deck'd with diamonds, and Indian stones;
> Not to be seen: my crown is call'd content;
> A crown it is that seldom kings enjoy.
>
> (3 *H. VI*, 3. 1. 62)

A child of God, King Henry died beseeching Heaven's pardon for his murderer:

> O, God forgive my sins, and pardon thee!
>
> (3 *H. VI*, 5. 6. 60)

*　　*　　*

At times this tragedy of errors won "teares" from "ten thousand spectators". But in

THE COMEDY OF ERRORS

which may have followed it the audience was invited to weep for mirth rather than for grief. Shakespeare turned Tragedy into Comedy by making the "outward" man a principal motive for the movement of the man "within". It is "the heavens", crook-backed Richard can say,

> that shap'd my body so;

and, to man's confusion, the heavens may sometimes shape one body of a man with the same features as another. A Puritan might frown at a girl for parading as a boy; and a sage perhaps at a masker who had mischievously imposed on a lady. But no one can censure an identical twin for resembling his fellow; and the more a pair of them puzzle themselves and their neighbours the pleasanter the comedy.

Yet tragic, like comic, effects may spring from no more than a man's bodily features; and in his study of man Shakespeare, unlike his laughing audience, may have been intent rather on the mischief than the mirth that may chance from men's innocent repetitions of one another. In this play there appears a woman who, in love with her husband (2. 2. 121) has yet grown jealous of a "love that drew him oft from home" (5. 1. 56). The mischief thus sown grows as she mistakes her husband's twin for himself.

Adriana	Ay, ay, Antipholus, look strange and frown:
	Some other mistress hath thy sweet aspects . . .
Ant. S.	What, was I married to her in my dream?
	Or sleep I now, and think I hear all this?
	What error drives our eyes and ears amiss?

(2. 2. 112)

Error succeeds error. Infected in his turn by the general confusion, the lady's real husband takes leave of his wits; and
"wronged" at last, in his conceit, "beyond imagination"
howls at his distracted consort:

> Dissembling harlot, thou art false in all,
> And art confederate with a damned pack
> To make a loathsome abject scorn of me:
> But with these nails I'll pluck out these false eyes,
> That would behold in me this shameful sport.
>
> (4. 4. 104)

It was not, however, the intention of Shakespeare to make
a tragedy of a comedy. To end all happily was easy enough
for him. The pair of twins had only to be seen together to
clear every cloud from the sky: and at a "gossips' feast" a
happily reunited family party heard at last "at large dis-
coursèd" their peculiar fortunes (5. 1. 395). The Comedy
remained a Comedy; and the audience dispersed perhaps with
merry tales of twins of their own acquaintance who had been
the occasion of similar, if not of even more remarkable,
occurrences.

*   *   *

Yet, if Shakespeare himself laughed at these drolleries, there
remained in him the disquiet of a man aware of the woes
engendered by men's irrational evil; and, ready to "vomit"
them, he could yield to the need to "ease his stomach with a
bitter tongue". In

TITUS ANDRONICUS

Shakespeare turned to study, with men the most "unnatural",
the unnatural evils born of their profligacy. No better than a
"wilderness of tigers" (3. 1. 54), Rome, like the "mad"
England of King Richard, appears as the resort of creatures

loveless; lustful; lying; lawless disintegrators of the State. In the Empress Tamora Shakespeare presents to his audience a being as outwardly bewitching as Queen Margaret, but inwardly as "flinty, rough, remorseless". Angry for the cruel death of her son at the hands of the Andronici (1. 1. 104) she'll "find a day to massacre them all" (1. 1. 450), and

> with her sacred wit
> To villany and vengeance consecrate (2. 1. 120)

assist her still surviving sons to ravish and dismember Titus's innocent daughter:

> Remember, boys, I pour'd forth tears in vain
> To save your brother from the sacrifice;
> But fierce Andronicus would not relent:
> Therefore, away with her, and use her as you will;
> The worse to her, the better lov'd of me. (2. 3. 163)

A woman who never "wags"

> But in her company there is a Moor (5. 2. 88),

Tamora was as lustful as she was remorseless—a wanton ready to pay "with twenty kisses" for tales of her paramour fit to startle a devil (5. 1. 120). No better than "a heinous tiger"— "her life was beastly and devoid of pity":

> No mournful bell shall ring her burial. (5. 3. 197)

If in Tamora Shakespeare has studied a woman as heartless as Margaret, in Aaron he has studied a man akin to King Richard. In him, in turn, the outward form twinned with the inner man: the one was no less black than the other.

> Now climbeth Tamora Olympus' top,
> Safe out of fortune's shot, and sits aloft . . .
> Then, Aaron, arm thy heart, and fit thy thoughts,
> To mount aloft with thy imperial mistress,

> And mount her pitch, whom thou in triumph long
> Hast prisoner held, fetter'd in amorous chains . . .
> Away with slavish weeds and servile thoughts!
> I will be bright, and shine in pearl and gold,
> To wait upon this new-made emperess.
> To wait, said I? to wanton with this queen,
> This goddess, this Semiramis, this nymph,
> This siren, that will charm Rome's Saturnine,
> And see his shipwreck and his commonweal's.
>
> (2. 1. 1)

Aaron is the source of all the varied sins of his inhuman confederates. His fiendish contrivances might have won him the
compliments of King Richard himself.

> Vengeance is in my heart, death in my hand,
> Blood and revenge are hammering in my head . . .
> This is the day of doom for Bassianus:
> His Philomel must lose her tongue to-day,
> Thy sons make pillage of her chastity,
> And wash their hands in Bassianus' blood.
>
> (2. 3. 38)

Irreligious, godless, conscienceless (5. 1. 73), Aaron is discovered at the last as at the first a creature quit of "all remorse
and nature". As lost as man may be, he is further even from
'himself' than Richard. No remorseful dreams of his dead
victims visit him; he sees no midnight ghosts; and in a cold
ecstasy sneers, at his end, at man's infantile follies:

> I am no baby, I, that with base prayers
> I should repent the evils I have done:
> Ten thousand worse than ever yet I did
> Would I perform, if I might have my will:
> If one good deed in all my life I did,
> I do repent it from my very soul. (5. 3. 185)

But—

> as the bark that hath discharg'd his fraught
> Returns with precious lading to the bay . . .
> Cometh Andronicus, bound with laurel boughs,
> To re-salute his country with his tears. (1. 1. 71)

In Titus Andronicus Shakespeare presents a man by nature noble; an old Roman;

> Patron of virtue, Rome's best champion; (1. 1. 65)

a conquering soldier that wished no better than "a staff of honour for his age"—

> But not a sceptre to control the world. (1. 1. 198)

Quiet in his home; thoughtful even for a "harmless fly" (3. 2. 63); Andronicus was the kind teacher of a child:

> Many a time he danc'd thee on his knee,
> Sung thee asleep, his loving breast thy pillow;
> Many a matter hath he told to thee,
> Meet and agreeing with thine infancy. (5. 3. 162)

Yet, thus endowed, Titus could show himself at times devoid of mercy (1. 1. 121); disposed to resent dishonour (1. 1. 340); and crossed—though by a son—as warm as any soldier:

> What, villain boy!
> Barr'st me my way in Rome? (*Stabbing him*) . . .
> Lucius   My lord, you are unjust; and, more than so,
> In wrongful quarrel you have slain your son.
> (1. 1. 290)

On the head of this old man, not always "with himself" (1. 1. 368), fell presently the furies of the pitiless Tamora and Aaron.

Tit.   Hear me, grave fathers! noble tribunes, stay!
For pity of mine age, whose youth was spent
In dangerous wars, whilst you securely slept . . .
Be pitiful to my condemned sons,
Whose souls are not corrupted as 'tis thought.

(3. 1. 1)

A third son banished, Titus can only weep again for the woes
of a raped daughter:

Speak, Lavinia, what accursed hand
Hath made thee handless in thy father's sight?

(3. 1. 66)

Alive to woes "as far from help as Limbo is from bliss"
(3. 1. 149), the father's sorrow for his child, losing its natural
bounds, grows inexplicable and "bottomless" (3. 1. 217):

If there were reason for these miseries,
Then into limits could I bind my woes:
When heaven doth weep, doth not the earth o'erflow?
If the winds rage, doth not the sea wax mad? . . .
And wilt thou have a reason for this coil?
I am the sea; hark, how her sighs do flow!
She is the weeping welkin, I the earth:
Then must my sea be moved with her sighs:
Then must my earth with her continual tears
Become a deluge, overflow'd and drowned:
For why, my bowels cannot hide her woes,
But like a drunkard must I vomit them.
Then give me leave; for losers will have leave
To ease their stomachs with their bitter tongues.

(3. 1. 220)

A woeful messenger appears with the heads of two of his
sons and his own severed hand:

Tit.   When will this fearful slumber have an end? . . .

38

Marcus	Now is a time to storm, why art thou still?
Tit.	Ha, ha, ha!
Mar.	Why dost thou laugh? it fits not with this hour.
Tit.	Why, I have not another tear to shed. (3. 1. 253)

'Justice' is gone from earth and sea and from the underworld; and, since there's none "in earth nor hell",

> We will solicit heaven, and move the gods
> To send down Justice for to wreak our wrongs.
>
> (4. 3. 50)

But the Justice of the gods is distant and Titus's Revenge at hand:

Titus (to Tamora's two sons)
> Hark, wretches, how I mean to martyr you.
> This one hand yet is left to cut your throats.
> Whilst that Lavinia 'tween her stumps doth hold
> The basin that receives your guilty blood . . .
> Hark villains! I will grind your bones to dust,
> And with your blood and it I'll make a paste . . .
> And bid that strumpet, your unhallow'd dam,
> Like to the earth, swallow her own increase,
> This is the feast that I have bid her to,
> And this the banquet she shall surfeit on. (5. 2. 181)

Shakespeare's audience, used as it was to sights of bloodshed, might view these horrors of the stage with eyes perhaps more fascinated than offended. But "tired with all these" Shakespeare himself may rather have wished for "restful death" as his anxious imagination enacted before him horrors more proper to Dante's *Inferno* or to a Belsen Camp than to man's sunny world. Yet on this lower "Limbo" of human unreason there fell for Shakespeare at times glimmers from the brighter world of human reason.

39

Marcus O brother, speak with possibility,
          And do not break into these deep extremes.
Tit.   Is not my sorrow deep, having no bottom?
          Then be my passions bottomless with them.
Mar.   But yet let reason govern thy lament. (3. 1. 215)

Marcus would teach his broken brother moderation (3. 2. 21) and, though capable himself of sudden passion (4. 3. 32), would as wisely urge his countrymen "by uproars sever'd" to knit

> These broken limbs again into one body (5. 3. 72);

that with men of his own kind he might in time contrive to

> order well the state,
> That like events may ne'er it ruinate. (5. 3. 203)

*   *   *

If Shakespeare's "bowels" suffered from Titus's trouble, he might yet be drawn by it to "ease his stomach" through conceiving of some remedy for it. Imagining a creature as unnatural as Aaron or Tamora, he could study whether such a monster might not cease to do evil and learn to do well. In a popular tale he discovered a woman of a sort to answer his purpose while amusing the public, and in

THE TAMING OF THE SHREW

he presents a creature in her own station not less "obdurate, flinty, rough and remorseless" than Tamora or Margaret, and yet a being capable, by suitable treatment, of developing the gentle disposition proper to woman. Katherina of Padua—

> young and beauteous,
> Brought up as best becomes a gentlewoman,
>   (1. 2. 86)

40

is yet a lady without cause peremptory; disdainful; violent; an "irksome, brawling scold" (1. 2. 188); a "fiend of hell" (1. 1. 88); her loving care—

> To comb your noddle with a three-legg'd stool,
> And paint your face, and use you like a fool.
>
> (1. 1. 64)

Revolting men of every age she is yet enough of a woman to be savagely envious of the gentle sister whose "beauteous modesty" (1. 2. 255) attracts the masculine throng like a magnet.

Kat. Of all thy suitors here I charge thee, tell
  Whom thou lov'st best: see thou dissemble not.
Bianca (*her hands tied*)
  Believe me, sister, of all the men alive
  I never yet beheld that special face
  Which I could fancy, more than any other.
Kat. Minion, thou liest. Is't not Hortensio?
Bia. If you affect him, sister, here I swear
  I'll plead for you myself, but you shall have him.
Kat. O then, belike, you fancy riches more:
  You will have Gremio to keep you fair.
Bia. Is it for him you do envy me so?
  Nay, then you jest, and now I well perceive
  You have but jested with me all this while:
  I prithee, sister Kate, untie my hands.
Kat. If that be jest, then all the rest was so. (*Strikes her*)
        (*Enter her father Baptista*)
Bap. Why, how now, dame! whence grows this
                              insolence? ...
Kat. Her silence flouts me, and I'll be revenged.
                      (*Flies after Bianca*)
Bap. What, in my sight? Bianca, get thee in.
                      (*Exit Bianca*)
Kat. What, will you not suffer me? Nay, now I see

41

> She is your treasure, she must have a husband;
> I must dance bare-foot on her wedding day . . .
> Talk not to me: I will go sit and weep,
> Till I can find occasion of revenge. (2. 1. 8)

Someone not less peremptory than this lady would seem to be needed to bring her to her sober woman's senses. A "great Hercules" (1. 2. 257) must undertake a labour not to be dreamed of by less strenuous persons. In Petruchio Shakespeare conceived of a male as firm "as mountains are for winds, that shake not, though they blow perpetually" (2. 1. 141).

> For I am he am born to tame you, Kate,
> And bring you from a wild Kate to a Kate
> Conformable as other household Kates. (2. 1. 278)

To the amusement of the audience Petruchio begins to disarm his hoyden by surprising her out of her wits:

Pet.   Father, 'tis thus: yourself and all the world,
That talk'd of her, have talk'd amiss of her . . .
For she's not froward, but modest as the dove;
She is not hot, but temperate as the morn . . .
And to conclude, we have 'greed so well together,
That upon Sunday is the wedding-day.

Kat.   I'll see thee hang'd on Sunday first . . .

Pet.   Be patient, gentlemen: I choose her for myself;
If she and I be pleas'd, what's that to you? . . .
I tell you, 'tis incredible to believe
How much she loves me: O, the kindest Kate!
She hung about my neck; and kiss on kiss
She vied so fast, protesting oath on oath,
That in a twink she won me to her love. (2. 1. 292)

In Church, Petruchio's violence dumbfounded the bride as much as her wondering guests:

Gremio Tut, she's a lamb, a dove, a fool to him!
      I'll tell you, Sir Lucentio: when the priest
      Should ask if Katherine should be his wife,
      'Ay, by gogs-wouns', quoth he; and swore so loud,
      That, all amaz'd, the priest let fall the book;
      And, as he stoop'd again to take it up,
      This mad-brain'd bridegroom took him such a cuff,
      That down fell priest and book, and book and priest:
      'Now take them up,' quoth he, 'if any list.'

(3. 2. 159)

At home Petruchio left the astounded Katherine "passing empty", and to "know her keeper's call" watched her as men watch kites,

      That bate, and beat, and will not be obedient;

(4. 1. 199)

and with a thousand tricks so tamed her will to follow his wit that at his word the sun became the moon for her (4.5.13) and an old gentleman a "lovely maid" (4. 5. 36). All "done in reverent care of her" (4. 1. 207), out of this wonder came at last, with a kind kiss (5. 1. 154), peace and love and quiet life,

      An awful rule, and right supremacy;
      And, to be short, what not, that's sweet and happy?

(5. 2. 108)

The fierce will of the Shrew stunned in her, Petruchio at last awoke in her the fair will of the woman.

      Women are soft, mild, pitiful and flexible.

(3 *H. VI*, 1. 4. 141)

The shrew gone out of her, her low woman's voice spoke at the last softly to Woman:

      Thy husband is thy lord, thy life, thy keeper . . .

43

> My mind hath been as big as one of yours,
> My heart as great, my reason haply more,
> To bandy word for word and frown for frown;
> But now I see our lances are but straws,
> Our strength as weak . . .   (5. 2. 146)

     ★ ★ ★

This fortunate reformation may have left Shakespeare with better hopes for man's unruly world; though the ladies of the audience he entertained may, perhaps, have quitted the theatre with certain misgivings. In happier mood the poet might now open his eyes again to his own more rational world of young men "glittering and sparkling Angels", and of maids "strange seraphic pieces of life and beauty"; and in

THE TWO GENTLEMEN OF VERONA

he seems to have toyed for a while with beauties of this description. In Valentine Shakespeare portrays "a proper man"; a being "beautified with goodly shape" (4. 1. 55); and, as innocent as fair, able to brook better than "flourishing peopled towns" a "shadowy desert, unfrequented woods" (5. 4. 2). Suspicious of love before love smiled at him (1. 1. 28), Valentine soon allows that

> Love's a mighty lord,
> And hath so humbled me, as I confess
> There is no woe to his correction,
> Nor to his service no such joy on earth.   (2. 4. 132)

In that service Valentine becomes a lover who, at one with his beloved, has learnt love's secret:

> She is my essence, and I leave to be,
> If I be not by her fair influence
> Foster'd, illumin'd, cherish'd, kept alive.   (3. 1. 182)

"A virtuous gentlewoman, mild and beautiful" (4. 4. 181),
Valentine's Silvia is in her turn a piece of natural "life and
beauty".

> Is she kind as she is fair?
>   For beauty lives with kindness:
> Love doth to her eyes repair,
>   To help him of his blindness,
> And, being help'd, inhabits there. (4. 2. 43)

As constant as Valentine, Silvia can fiercely chide a faithless
lover from her:

> Thou subtle, perjur'd, false, disloyal man!
> Think'st thou I am so shallow, so conceitless,
> To be seduced by thy flattery,
> That hast deceiv'd so many with thy vows?
>   (4. 2. 92)

Enforced by her father to marry "vain Thurio" (4. 3. 16), she
can only say good-bye to home and lovelessness:

> Sir Eglamour, I would to Valentine,
> To Mantua . . .
> Urge not my father's anger, Eglamour,
> But think upon my grief, a lady's grief,
> And on the justice of my flying hence,
> To keep me from a most unholy match,
> Which heaven and fortune still rewards with plagues.
>   (4. 3. 22)

As constant as these lovers there appears on the stage another
piece of "life and beauty". Julia would follow her Proteus as
closely as Silvia her Valentine.

> A true-devoted pilgrim is not weary
> To measure kingdoms with his feeble steps,
> Much less shall she that hath Love's wings to fly,

> And when the flight is made to one so dear,
> Of such divine perfection as Sir Proteus. (2. 7. 9)

Julia's love was not to need her waiting-woman's admonition
to—

> qualify the fire's extreme rage,
> Lest it should burn above the bounds of reason.
>
> (2. 7. 22)

Finding her Proteus "subtle, perjur'd, false, disloyal", she was
rather to pity than to seek vengeance on him.

> Alas, poor fool, why do I pity him? . . .
> Because I love him, I must pity him. (4. 4. 94)

In Katherine the Shrew Shakespeare had watched the raising
of a woman, but in Julia's Proteus he was to watch rather the
fall of a man—an unnatural "apostasy" in him. "A votary to
fond desire" (1. 1. 52), Sir Proteus appears on the stage a lover
as constant as Valentine:

> Here is my hand, for my true constancy;
> And when that hour o'erslips me in the day
> Wherein I sigh not, Julia, for thy sake,
> The next ensuing hour some foul mischance
> Torment me for my love's forgetfulness! (2. 2. 8)

Not unsuspected however by a waiting maid (2. 7. 79) and a
man servant (3. 1. 261), Proteus was no sooner off from his
ulia than he was after his Valentine's Silvia:

> O, but I love his lady too too much! . . .
> 'Tis but her picture I have yet beheld,
> And that hath dazzled my reason's light;
> But when I look on her perfections,
> There is no reason but I shall be blind.
> If I can check my erring love, I will;
> If not, to compass her I'll use my skill. (2. 4. 201)

Become a plotter as clever in his different station as King
Richard (2. 6), Proteus might have been expected to be
troubled at last by such nightmares of a guilty conscience as
disturbed that sinner. But to Shakespeare in his rational mood
evil in man appeared so "unnatural" that Proteus was to
repent as quickly as he sinned:

> My shame and guilt confounds me,
> Forgive me, Valentine: if hearty sorrow
> Be a sufficient ransom for offence,
> I tender't here: I do as truly suffer
> As e'er I did commit.   (5. 4. 73)

Valentine is as ready to forgive as Proteus to repent:

> By penitence the Eternal's wrath's appeas'd:
> And, that my love may appear plain and free,
> All that was mine in Silvia I give thee.   (5. 4. 81)

More exuberant than exact, Valentine's offer left Julia fainting;
but Silvia rather . . . smiling quietly (5. 4. 84; cf. *M. of V.*,
4. 1. 282–289). Proteus happily recovered his love for his
Julia as Valentine constantly maintained his love for his Silvia.
For a moment Shakespeare seems to smile at a world restored
to its reason, and to the peace and beauty natural to it.

> Come, let us go, we will include all jars
> With triumphs, mirth, and rare solemnity.
> (5. 4. 160)

THE STATESMAN

CHAPTER II

THE STATESMAN

SHAKESPEARE'S study, in these plays, of man's social behaviour may have left him still doubtful of the character of
the remedy which might "through and through cleanse the
foul body of the infected world". It was open to him, however, to follow the man of science in a parallel predicament.
From his study of the chaos of the physical world the man of
science derives hypotheses of a kind to serve for its remedy;
and Shakespeare's study of the not less complicated chaos of
the world of man could furnish him with hypotheses of a
kind to serve, in their turn, to recover it. In Henry the Sixth
had appeared a being "famed for mildness, peace, and prayer".
Henry however was of a nature that, sufficient for a people of
innocents needing "no name of magistrate", was more ready
to retire from an evil world than to take arms against its
troubles—a man, accordingly, to some—

> Whose bookish rule hath pull'd fair England down.
> (2 *H. VI*, 1. 1. 257)

Men more conversant than himself with the world appeared,
on the other hand, apt, like King Richard, to be creatures of
passion too energetically fond of themselves to be in love with
mankind; or, like the Shrew, too scornful of it to be its ready
assistants. In men like Lucius and Marcus Shakespeare however had met with beings of a kind to unite with a life of
activity in the world an interest in its health and well-being;

48

men of a will "to knit these broken limbs again into one body"; and so to "order the state

> That like events may ne'er it ruinate.

The Idealism of a Henry might thus seem a medicine useful to man only as man's empirical experience was combined with it (*Two Gent.*, 1. 3. 20). "To suck the sweets of sweet philosophy" must be approved by the physician:

> Only, good master, while we do admire
> This virtue, and this moral discipline,
> Let's be no stoics nor no stocks, I pray;
> Or so devote to Aristotle's checks
> As Ovid be an outcast quite abjur'd.
> (*The Shrew*, 1. 1. 28)

Ovid united with Aristotle might be a medicine of a kind to keep men close to the world; while Aristotle united with Ovid might possibly keep men virtuous in it. A being who had imbibed this mixture might learn to command his passions without becoming a recluse; and happily mingling "blood" with "judgement" might find in a 'mean' between dispassion and passion a virtue serviceable to the world. A man of this temper might presently become a Statesman and, like Aristotle's 'Phronimos', find in his care for man the natural purpose of his existence.

Like the Roman Marcus shunning "deep extremes" (*T.A.*, 3. 1. 216), the 'Statesman', in public or private, might thus be conceived the physician competent to "cleanse the foul body of the infected world". Just; unblinded by irrational passion; clear of sight and therefore efficient; such a man—though likely enough to be misunderstood by men of slighter wit than himself—could be expected to win the ears of his people; and, faithfully followed by it, in good time to secure its health

49

and well-being. Shakespeare was indeed not unaware that the prescriptions of the Statesman might be as fallible as those of the doctor. Either might learn by his skill to "prophesy, with a near aim, of the main chance of things" (2 *H. IV*, 3. 1. 82). But no skill of man is able to cope with all the baffling vicissitudes of men and of Society (2 *H. IV*, 3. 1. 45). As a theatrical "Johannes Factotum" Shakespeare may himself have known, with the frown of the Statesman, the troubling presence of the "worldly chances and mishaps" (*T.A.*, 1. 1. 152) that must attend his onerous calling. The value of the Statesman must still remain a question to be patiently scrutinized; though Shakespeare may rightly have concluded that

> it never yet did hurt
> To lay down likelihoods and forms of hope.
>> (2 *H. IV*, 1. 3. 34)

In his play—

LOVE'S LABOUR'S LOST

Shakespeare seems to be studying with a good deal of humour the labourings of minds capable of giving birth in their time to the politic being he is looking for. To an audience perhaps of noblemen Shakespeare here presents a King "at war against his own affections"

> And the huge army of the world's desires. (1. 1. 10)

Purposing to make his Court "a little Academe", he has united with him "fellow-scholars" ready "not to see a woman" for three years,

> And one day in a week to touch no food . . .
> And then, to sleep but three hours in the night;
>> (1. 1. 37)

the sweetest "recreation" of these gentlemen being to listen
to a man

> That hath a mint of phrases in his brain:
> One whom the music of his own vain tongue
> Doth ravish like enchanting harmony. (1. 1. 163)

Devoted thus "to Aristotle's checks", these "brave conquerors" (1. 1. 8) were however forgetful of the 'Ovid'
hidden in them.

> A maid of grace and complete majesty (1. 1. 135)

descended, with three other Graces, unavoidably on them,
and in a moment the four Stoic "stocks" became as many fond
lovers; quite abjured their Aristotle; and fell, forsworn, from
the extreme of asceticism into the extreme of doting.

King Ay me! ...
> O queen of queens! how far dost thou excel,
> No thought can think, nor tongue of mortal tell.
>> (4. 3. 21)

Longa- O sweet Maria, empress of my love! ...
ville A woman I forswore, but I will prove,
> Thou being a goddess, I forswore not thee.
>> (4. 3. 54)

Dumaine I would forget her, but a fever she
> Reigns in my blood, and will remember'd be.
>> (4. 3. 93)

For ever jesting, the fourth of the Stoics, "whip" at once of
love and of hypocrisy, derides the breakers of vows maintained unflinchingly by himself:

Berowne When shall you see me write a thing in rhyme?
> Or groan for love? ... When shall you hear that I

> Will praise a hand, a foot, a face, an eye,
> A gait, a state, a brow, a breast, a waist,
> A leg, a limb? (4. 3. 179)

Yet, boast as he might, the mocker Berowne had been the first of the Stoics to feel Cupid's shameful enticements.

Ber. Guilty, my lord, guilty! I confess, I confess.
King What?
Ber. That you three fools lack'd me fool to make up the mess. (4. 3. 203)

Shakespeare may never have known a beauty so outwardly alluring as his own "dark lady"; and it is to a beauty of this fascinating quality that he yokes the reluctant Berowne. As little devoted by nature to women as the Shrew was to men, the lover's irritation can at first compare his innocent captor to—

> a German clock,
> Still a-repairing, ever out of frame . . .
> A whitely wanton, with a velvet brow,
> With two pitch-balls stuck in her face for eyes,
> Ay, and, by heaven, one that will do the deed
> Though Argus were her eunuch and her guard.
> (3. 1. 184)

Unwillingly attached to his Siren through a passion he had once made his jest, Berowne can only groan:

> Go to; it is a plague
> That Cupid will impose for my neglect
> Of his almighty dreadful little might.
> Well, I will love, write, sigh, pray, sue and groan;
> Some men must love my lady, and some Joan.
> (3. 1. 195)

Whether black or white the stranger-ladies were however less in need than their lovers of an Argus to watch their proceedings. So far from humouring their lovers they were as intent on humbling them as Petruchio on humbling his Katherine. Berowne's now "heavenly Rosaline" (4. 3. 219; 4. 3. 297) was as forward as the rest in the merry-making. Anxious to make their lovers "fawn and beg and seek" (5. 2. 62), their merriment diverted themselves as much as it distracted their bewilderd admirers.

Ros. But shall we dance, if they desire us to't?
Princess No, to the death we will not move a foot,
  Nor to their penn'd speech render we no grace;
  But while 'tis spoke each turn away her face . . .
  So shall we stay, mocking intended game,
  And they, well mock'd, depart away with shame.
          (5. 2. 145)

Thus shamed, the "breed of wits so wonder'd at" became but "tapers" that "sweet breaths puff'd out":

Prin. Will they not, think you, hang themselves tonight?
  Or ever, but in vizards, show their faces?
  This pert Berowne was out of countenance quite.
Ros. O, they were all in lamentable cases! (5. 2. 266)

Yet these ladies were to prove themselves in the end, like Petruchio, rather tutors than tormentors, rather physicians than termagants. The merriment ends with the news of a father's death (5. 2. 709); and to her royal lover—begging as she takes a hurried leave of him—

  Now at the latest minute of the hour,
  Grant us your loves (5. 2. 777)

the Princess gives the needful physic:

  If for my love . . .
  You will do aught, this shall you do for me:
  Your oath I will not trust, but go with speed

> To some forlorn and naked hermitage,
> Remote from all the pleasures of the world . . .
> If this austere insociable life
> Change not your offer made in heat of blood . . .
> But that it bear this trial, and last love;
> Then, at the expiration of the year,
> Come challenge me . . .
> And, by this virgin palm now kissing thine,
> I will be thine. (5. 2. 782)

The triumphant 'Ovid' in the King that had abjured the 'Aristotle' at first vaunted by him is, by the Princess's prescription, to be now restrained and qualified by Aristotle—while not forgotten, to be tempered and made rational and constant in him; from the "doting" of a Proteus to be raised into the "love" of a Valentine. If the 'mean' of love is thus to take the place in the King of the 'extremes' of passion and chilliness, a larger love is to replace the egoism of another sinner of the party. A different medicine is to be prescribed for a different ailment. Repudiating her first glib opinion of her lover (2. 1. 66)—"You must be purgèd too", says Doctor Rosaline.

> You are attaint with faults and perjury . . .
> The world's large tongue
> Proclaims you for a man replete with mocks . . .
> Which you on all estates will execute
> That lie within the mercy of your wit.
> To weed this wormwood from your fruitful brain,
> And therewithal to win me, if you please, . . .
> You shall this twelvemonth term from day to day
> Visit the speechless sick, and still converse
> With groaning wretches; and your task shall be,
> With all the fierce endeavour of your wit
> To enforce the pained impotent to smile.
>
> (5. 2. 808, 832)

To jest for others' sake rather than for his own is the sour prescription the pitiless "shrew" Berowne consents to try with a view to making his sweet lady "joyful of his reformation":

> A twelvemonth? well; befall what will befall,
> I'll jest a twelvemonth in an hospital.   (5. 2. 860)

*   *   *

By leaving the world these gallants of Navarre were thus to return to it men sobered, constant, of service in the human 'hospital'; physicians then, it might be, skilled to "cleanse the foul body of the infected world". The parts the physician may play in the world are as manifold as the maladies that trouble the health of mankind, and the dramatist must choose from among their endless variety the most likely to hold the attention of his audience. In

ROMEO AND JULIET

Shakespeare presents "Two households" that "from ancient grudge break to new mutiny".

Prince   What, ho! you men, you beasts,
That quench the fire of your pernicious rage
With purple fountains issuing from your veins ...
Three civil brawls, bred of an airy word,
By thee, old Capulet, and Montague,
Have thrice disturb'd the quiet of our streets ...
If ever you disturb our streets again,
Your lives shall pay the forfeit of the peace.
                                        (1. 1. 90)

In these streets wandered a disconsolate lover: a man in doting love with a beauty of the same name and presence as Berowne's bewildering Rosaline. "Planting oblivion, beating reason back" (*V. and A.*, l. 557), passion has estranged him from 'himself' and made a madman rather than a man of him.

Tut, I have lost myself; I am not here;
This is not Romeo, he's some other where.

(1. 1. 203)

As inconstant as the moon, doting is a passion that "alters
with brief hours and weeks" (*Son.* 116); and Romeo is no
sooner desired to "examine other beauties" (1. 1. 234), than,
forgetting his love for Rosaline, he readily finds 'himself' in
a girl (1. 5. 46) that, though of the rival household, finds
'herself' as much in Romeo (1. 5. 136):

Juliet	In truth, fair Montague, I am too fond;
	And therefore thou mayst think my 'haviour light:
	But trust me, gentleman, I'll prove more true
	Than those that have more cunning to be strange.
	I should have been more strange, I must confess,
	But that thou overheard'st, ere I was ware,
	My true love's passion; therefore pardon me,
	And not impute this yielding to light love,
	Which the dark night hath so discovered.
Rom.	Lady, by yonder blessed moon I swear,
	That tips with silver all these fruit-tree tops,—
Juliet	O, swear not by the moon, th' inconstant moon,
	That monthly changes in her circled orb,
	Lest that thy love prove likewise variable.
Rom.	What shall I swear by?
Jul.	Do not swear at all;
	Or, if thou wilt, swear by thy gracious self,
	Which is the god of my idolatry,
	And I'll believe thee . . .
	My bounty is as boundless as the sea,
	My love as deep; the more I give to thee,
	The more I have, for both are infinite.

(2. 2. 98)

Thus "one" with Romeo, as he with her, Juliet can no more

part from him than he from Juliet: married they must be—
fearful as they may be that this nocturnal contract is

> too rash, too unadvised, too sudden,
> Too like the lightning which doth cease to be
> Ere one can say 'It lightens'.   (2. 2. 118)

In this predicament Romeo however is not without the
thought of an adviser, of an expert helper in the hour of
trouble:

> Hence will I to my ghostly father's cell,
> His help to crave and my dear hap to tell.
>
> (2. 2. 189)

Romeo's "ghostly father" was a philosopher able to
moralize in the earliest morning. Father Laurence cannot fill
his osier-case without considering the enigmatic powers and
virtues of man's singular universe:

> O, mickle is the powerful grace that lies
> In herbs, plants, stones, and their true qualities:
> For naught so vile that on the earth doth live,
> But to the earth some special good doth give;
> Nor naught so good, but, strain'd from that fair use,
> Revolts from true birth, stumbling on abuse:
> Virtue itself turns vice, being misapplied,
> And vice sometime's by action dignified . . .
> Two such opposed kings encamp them still
> In man as well as herbs, grace and rude will;
> And where the worser is predominant,
> Full soon the canker death eats up that plant.
>
> (2. 3. 15)

Less attractive to the playgoer than to the philosopher, the
Friar is yet a man beloved in his own city; "a holy man"
(5. 3. 270) commonly resorted to; as conversant with the

world as with Heaven; experienced; no teasing tutor like
Petruchio but providing the medicine of moderation against
man's dangerous excesses (2. 6. 9).   Listening to Romeo's
pleading cry—

<blockquote>

both our remedies
Within thy help and holy physic lies,   (2. 3. 51)
</blockquote>

he answers his patient with the pertinent query—

<blockquote>

Is Rosaline, that thou didst love so dear,
So soon forsaken? . . .

Rom.   Thou chid'st me oft for loving Rosaline.

Fri.   For doting, not for loving, pupil mine . . .

Rom.   I pray thee, chide not; she whom I love now
Doth grace for grace and love for love allow;
The other did not so.

Fri.   O, she knew well
Thy love did read by rote and could not spell.
But come, young waverer, come, go with me,
In one respect I'll thy assistant be;
For this alliance may so happy prove,
To turn your households' rancour to pure love.
</blockquote>

(2. 3. 66)

The hope of the wisest physician may however be undone
by an accident. A new "mutiny" in the streets of Verona called
forth the Prince again:

<blockquote>

Where are the vile beginners of this fray?

Benvolio O noble prince, I can discover all
The unlucky manage of this fatal brawl:
There lies the man—slain by young Romeo—
That slew thy kinsman, brave Mercutio. . . .

Prin.   Romeo slew him, he slew Mercutio:
Who now the price of this dear blood doth owe?

Mont.   Not Romeo, prince, he was Mercutio's friend;
</blockquote>

> His fault concludes but what the law should end,
> The life of Tybalt.

Prin.   And for that offence
> Immediately we do exile him hence . . .
> Nor tears nor prayers shall purchase out abuses:
> Therefore use none: let Romeo hence in haste,
> Else, when he's found, that hour is his last. . . .
>   (3. 1. 146)

Rom.   Ha, banishment! be merciful, say 'death';
> For exile hath more terror in his look,
> Much more than death: do not say 'banishment'.
>   (3. 3. 12)

As troubled as Romeo, Juliet finds Life itself in exile with him from the world:

> 'Romeo is banished:' to speak that word
> Is father, mother, Tybalt, Romeo, Juliet,
> All slain, all dead: (3. 2. 122)

the 'one' they were, made 'two', "no words can that woe sound" (3. 2. 126).

To the cry of the distracted Romeo that "every cat and dog" may look on Juliet, "but Romeo may not" (3. 3. 30), the frowning physician however is to answer with the sting of the surgeon:

Fri.   Thou fond mad man, hear me but speak a word.
Rom. O, thou wilt speak again of banishment.
Fri.   I'll give thee armour to keep off that word;
> Adversity's sweet milk, philosophy,
> To comfort thee, though thou art banished.
Rom. Yet 'banished'? Hang up philosophy! . . .
Fri.   O, then I see that madmen have no ears. . ..
> What, rouse thee, man! thy Juliet is alive,
> For whose dear sake thou wast but lately dead
> There thou art happy: Tybalt would kill thee,

But thou slew'st Tybalt; there art thou happy too:
The law, that threaten'd death, became thy friend,
And turns it to exile; there art thou happy . . .
Go, get thee to thy love, as was decreed,
Ascend her chamber, hence and comfort her.
But look thou stay not till the watch be set,
For then thou canst not pass to Mantua . . .
Sojourn in Mantua; I'll find out your man,
And he shall signify from time to time
Every good hap to you that chances here:
Give me thy hand: 'tis late; farewell; good night.

Rom. But that a joy past joy calls out on me,
It were a grief, so brief to part with thee.
Farewell. (3. 3. 52)

An unknown 'wife' in sudden danger of a suitor (3. 5. 113)
Juliet in her turn runs to the Friar for a remedy more apt to
her peculiar case than her false Nurse's remedy to "marry"
with the "lovely county", Paris (3. 5. 219).

Jul. O, shut the door, and when thou hast done so,
Come weep with me; past hope, past cure, past help!
Fri. Ah, Juliet, I already know thy grief . . .
Jul. Tell me not, friar, that thou hear'st of this,
Unless thou tell me how I may prevent it . . .
Therefore, out of thy long-experienced time,
Give me some present counsel . . .
Be not so long to speak; I long to die,
If what thou speak'st speak not of remedy.
Fri. Hold, daughter: I do spy a kind of hope,
Which craves as desperate an execution
As that is desperate which we would prevent . . .
To-morrow night look that thou lie alone,
Let not thy nurse lie with thee in thy chamber:
Take thou this vial, being then in bed,
And this distilled liquor drink thou off:

> When presently through all thy veins shall run
> A cold and drowsy humour . . .
> Each part, deprived of supple government,
> Shall, stiff and stark and cold, appear like death:
> And in this borrow'd likeness of shrunk death
> Thou shalt continue two and forty hours,
> And then awake as from a pleasant sleep . . .
> Then, as the manner of our country is . . .
> Thou shalt be borne to that same ancient vault
> Where all the kindred of the Capulets lie.
> In the mean time, against thou shalt awake,
> Shall Romeo by my letters know our drift;
> And hither shall he come; and he and I
> Will watch thy waking, and that very night
> Shall Romeo bear thee hence to Mantua . . .

Jul. Give me, give me! O, tell not me of fear!

Fri. Hold; get you gone, be strong and prosperous
In this resolve: I'll send a friar with speed
To Mantua, with my letters to thy lord.

Jul. Love give me strength! and strength shall help afford.
Farewell, dear father! (4. 1. 44)

Yet Heaven, that men call 'chance', was once again to overrule the skill of its servant. Intent on bringing peace to the city through the union of the lovers, the Friar's practical wisdom seemed to be finally cheated of its righteous intention.

> A greater power than we can contradict
> Hath thwarted our intents. (5. 3. 153)

False news of Juliet's death was carried to Romeo (5. 1. 20); the true was not to reach him (5. 2. 13). In a tomb, dewed with the blood of Paris, the lovers met for the last time:

Rom.   Eyes, look your last!
Arms, take your last embrace! and, lips, O you
The doors of breath, seal with a righteous kiss

> A dateless bargain to engrossing death!
> Come, bitter conduct, come, unsavoury guide!
> Thou desperate pilot, now at once run on
> The dashing rocks thy sea-sick weary bark.
> Here's to my love! O true apothecary!
> Thy drugs are quick. Thus with a kiss I die.
>
> (5. 3. 112)

And Juliet—too late awaking:

> What's here? a cup, closed in my true love's hand?
> Poison, I see, hath been his timeless end:
> O churl! drunk all, and left no friendly drop
> To help me after? I will kiss thy lips;
> Haply some poison yet doth hang on them,
> To make me die with a restorative.
> Thy lips are warm . . .
> Yea, noise? then I'll be brief. O happy dagger
> This is thy sheath; there rust, and let me die.
>
> (5. 3. 161)

Before the Prince—roused by a new crying in the streets—appeared the downcast Friar:

> If aught in this
> Miscarried by my fault, let my old life
> Be sacrificed some hour before his time
> Unto the rigour of severest law. (5. 3. 266)

Dismayed as he might be, yet the earthly sage was not to go uncomforted. Not the life but the death of the lovers was by Heaven's prerogative decreed to turn the city's "rancour" to "pure love"; Only "their misadventured piteous overthrow" could "with their death bury their parents' strife" (*Pro.* l. 7).

> *Cap.* O brother Montague, give me thy hand:
> This is my daughter's jointure, for no more
> Can I demand.

Mon.   But I can give thee more:
        For I will raise her statue in pure gold.   (5. 3. 296)

*   *   *

The "immortal part" of Romeo and Juliet might "breathe
still with angels" (5. 1. 19). But to breathing creatures of
earth their dim bodies could bring only woe:

Prince   A glooming peace this morning with it brings.
                                        (5. 3. 305)

To steer man's course to fortune (1. 4. 112) an omniscient
Providence would seem a more capable pilot than the un-
certain skill of a poor Friar. To incarnate a heavenly Power
in a mere man might however appear a venturesome proceeding to a human audience, and, avoiding things "that will
never please" (*M.N.D.*, 3. 1. 10), Shakespeare resolved, it
seems, to play the poet rather with imagination's

        shaping fantasies that apprehend
    More than cool reason ever comprehends.
                            (*M.N.D.*, 5. 1. 5)

Smiling, yet "selling cheap" perhaps "what is most dear", in

A MIDSUMMER NIGHT'S DREAM

Shakespeare conceived of a Power which, enclosed in the
opportune form of a Fairy King, might seem as intelligible as
it was amusing to a courtly audience. Endowed with powers
of heaven (3. 2. 355), Oberon is not without concern for the
affairs of men. Lord of Fairyland, like his minister Puck he is
ready also to be both "auditor" and "actor" in the world of
mankind (3. 1. 81). In this world live Lysander—a new
Valentine—in constant love with the fair Hermia; Demetrius
—a Proteus—whose love for Helena fades as it blossoms for
Hermia; Helena, sighing, like Julia, for a faithless lover;

Hermia, as constant as Silvia, yet doomed by Duke Theseus, to die "for disobedience to your father's will, or else to wed Demetrius, as he would" (1. 1. 87).

The course of true love never did run smooth

(1. 1. 134)

and its torrents presently bore the several lovers into the woods where Oberon was watching (1. 1. 208–251).

Oberon himself was not without experience of the troubles of love. His Queen Titania was, at times, hardly less trying to her Lord than Juno could be to her Jove.

Tit.   Why art thou here,
     Come from the farthest steppe of India?
     But that, forsooth, the bouncing Amazon,
     Your buskin'd mistress and your warrior love,
     To Theseus must be wedded, and you come
     To give their bed joy and prosperity.
Obe.   How canst thou thus for shame, Titania,
     Glance at my credit with Hippolyta,
     Knowing I know thy love to Theseus? (2. 1. 68)

As willing as the perversest of wives to "cross her Oberon" (2. 1. 119), Titania however was to rue it for refusing him "a little changeling boy" to be his "henchman" (2. 1. 120). The possessor of a magical "juice" as potent as Juliet's strange drug, Oberon was to make merry with Titania.

                Having once this juice,
I'll watch Titania when she is asleep,
And drop the liquor of it in her eyes.
The next thing then she waking looks upon,
Be it on lion, bear, or wolf, or bull,
On meddling monkey, or on busy ape,
She shall pursue it with the soul of love:
And ere I take this charm from off her sight,

As I can take it with another herb,
I'll make her render up her page to me. (2. 1. 176)

The next thing that Titania was to look on was, through
Puck's ingenious manipulation, nothing better than a human
weaver with an ass's head (3. 2. 17); a monster she must
"madly dote on" (2. 1. 171) till Oberon's other herb had,
with the sight, restored the feelings proper to a Fairy Queen.

A medicine of such likely use for bringing Titania to her
senses could be nothing but useful in curing the trouble of
a human lover. The eyes of the faithless Demetrius had only
to be anointed with the heavenly juice for him to regain his
lost love for his Helena. Fortune however was to favour
Oberon's Puck as little as it had favoured the fallible Friar
Laurence:

Obe.   Thou hast mistaken quite,
And laid the love-juice on some true-love's sight:
Of thy misprision must perforce ensue
Some true love turn'd, and not a false turn'd true.
                                          (3. 2. 88)

Through the potency of Oberon's charm and the chances of
fortune it so fell out that Hermia incredibly lost her two lovers
and the lover-less Helena as incredibly won them. None of
the lovers continued to understand the words of the others;
and saner sounds scattered through the forest from Theseus'
pack of hounds (4. 1. 111) than from the passionate gibberings
of the bewildered humans. Infecting the love of man and
woman the strange juice infected as dreadfully the love of
woman for woman:

Helena   O, is all forgot?
All school-days' friendship, childhood innocence?
We, Hermia, like two artificial gods,
Have with our needles created both one flower,

> Both on one sampler, sitting on one cushion,
> Both warbling of one song, both in one key;
> As if our hands, our sides, voices, and minds,
> Had been incorporate. So we grew together,
> Like to a double cherry, seeming parted,
> But yet an union in partition;
> Two lovely berries moulded on one stem . . .
> And will you rent our ancient love asunder,
> To join with men in scorning your poor friend?
> It is not friendly, 'tis not maidenly:
> Our sex, as well as I, may chide you for it,
> Though I alone do feel the injury.   (3. 2. 201)

Gentler than Hermia, Helena can only weep her weary womanhood (3. 2. 301); but Hermia, "fierce", when vexed, "though she be but little" (3. 2. 325) can at last break wildly out:

> How low am I, thou painted maypole? speak;
> How low am I? I am not yet so low
> But that my nails can reach unto thine eyes.
> > (3. 2. 296)

Troubled however as men might be, nothing in the end was to prove too much for the skill of the practical Oberon. With the good purpose and more than the power of Friar Laurence he proceeded to set things right as well for his own whimsical world as for the world of suffering mortals.

Obe.   Now, my Titania; wake you, my sweet queen.
Tit.   My Oberon! what visions have I seen!
    Methought I was enamoured of an ass. (4. 1. 80)

Waking like one from a dream, Lysander finds his love for Hermia his own again; Demetrius, his withered love for Helena in flower again (4. 1. 170).

With league whose date till death shall never end
(3. 2. 373)

the now wide-awake lovers find their way back, with the
awakened "ass", to Athens.

Obe.   There shall the pairs of faithful lovers be
          Wedded, with Theseus, all in jollity.   (4. 1. 96)

*   *   *

An audience assured that it had "but slumber'd, while these
visions did appear" might perhaps retire without requiring
an "amends" for its idleness (5. 1. 432). To Shakespeare, however, conscious that dreams are but "the children of an idle
brain" (*R. and J.*, 1. 4. 97), this play may have seemed a "very
midsummer madness" (*Twelfth Night*, 3. 4. 55); a thing as insubstantial as an iridescent bubble. To "cleanse the foul body
of the infected world", dreams must give way to sterner
Reality, and a Man take the place of the King of the Fairies
as the physician of human disorders. Through such a man the
State might be conceived to pass from sickness to health; from
deformity to beauty. A man cannot fondle a State as he may
fondle a woman; yet to one aware that the well-being of men
depends on the health of the State, a State in health must look
a thing of beauty; and the composer of a State a greater artist
than the composer of a fable (cf. *Hamlet*, 3. 3. 8–23). If a
poetry of 'action' must thus be expected of a King earnest for
the State's well-being, a King of contrasting endowment may
be as readily imagined:—a poet of fancy rather than of action
who lives, a dreamer, in a cloud, rather than a physician, in
the actual world of suffering humanity: a visionary like "the
lover and the poet" (*M.N.D.*, 5. 1. 2–22); a player readier
to please men's eyes and ears than to comfort the lives of a
people. Reigning through the grace of Heaven rather than

67

their own, such inexpert physicians of the State are not unknown to history, and in

KING RICHARD II

Shakespeare seems to be studying a ruler of this description. Presented at first to his audience as a man who admits himself to be "no physician", yet who is skilled enough to prescribe the sovereign remedy for social disorder—

> Forget, forgive; conclude and be agreed,
>
> (1. 1. 156)

Richard is presently discovered to be patient rather than physician; an invalid who has carelessly committed his sickness to the care of physicians whose art can only aggravate the disorders it has produced in him (2. 1. 97). Surrounded by "a thousand flatterers" (2. 1. 100); careless of the good counsel even of a dying prophet (2. 1); "the king is not himself" (2. 1. 241):

> The commons hath he pill'd with grievous taxes,
> And quite lost their hearts: the nobles hath he fined
> For ancient quarrels, and quite lost their hearts.
>
> (2. 1. 246)

His England, "bound in with the triumphant sea" is, under him, a land "bound in with shame" (2. 1. 61); a "drooping country" with "a broken wing" (2. 1. 292); a wilderness; a desolation.

Gardener   O, what pity is it
> That he had not so trimm'd and dress'd his land
> As we this garden! . . .
> Had he done so to great and growing men,
> They might have lived to bear and he to taste
> Their fruits of duty. (3. 4. 55)

The difficulties which gathered round Richard might have tempted the 'gardener' in him to grapple with, and, if he could, to end them. But so far were his troubles from awaking in Richard the true man of action that they rather aroused in him the man of "imagination all compact". Thoughts as dream-like as the fairy Peaseblossom ran rioting in Richard: thoughts, in peace, charming to poets and ladies; but in danger dreadful to the thwarted man of action:

> My lord, wise men ne'er sit and wail their woes,
> But presently prevent the ways to wail.
>
> (3. 2. 178; 3. 2. 29)

Inactive in the world, Richard's energy was expended in peopling his fancy with dream-bred worlds invisible to human reason:—an Earth whose "armèd" stones shall save his threatened throne (3. 2. 24); a Heaven whose Omnipotent Power shall utterly prostrate his enemies:

> Yet know, my master, God omnipotent,
> Is mustering in his clouds on our behalf
> Armies of pestilence; and they shall strike
> Your children yet unborn and unbegot,
> That lift your vassal hands against my head,
> And threat the glory of my precious crown.
>
> (3. 3. 85; 3. 2. 60)

"Sad stories of the death of kings" (3. 2. 156); dreams of the fate approaching himself (3. 3. 147) form the "idle" tales (3. 3. 171), the "senseless conjurations" (3. 2. 23), he confesses to without the power to control them (5. 5. 47–49). Vexed by a world of which he was never a native, Richard could only allow—

> They well deserve to have,
> That know the strong'st and surest way to get.
>
> (3. 3. 200)

Divine as Heaven's gift of a crown may be, it cannot weigh with a man's own wisdom in the rule of a people; and a wise man without that gift is of more service to a State than a fool with it. With "the sick hour" that Richard's "surfeit made" (2. 2. 84), there appeared in the vexed State an uncrowned physician of more promise than Richard. No idle man of dreams, he was not one to let imagination rule his reason:

> O, who can hold a fire in his hand
> By thinking on the frosty Caucasus?
> Or cloy the hungry edge of appetite
> By bare imagination of a feast? (1. 3. 294)

Bolingbroke appears as a youth "Not sick, although I have to do with death, But lusty, young and cheerly drawing breath" (1. 3. 65); a good companion (2. 3. 6); courteous to the people (1. 4. 24); kind to the Queen (3. 1. 37); pardoning where he may (4. 1. 87; 5. 3. 131). Accepting, at last, the crown laid down by "plume-pluck'd" Richard, he yet remained as a Statesman still troubled by the deposition, and the death (5. 6. 34), of an anointed Sovereign. A good physician may look sourer sometimes than a useless one, and, like the good gardener, laboriously lop "superfluous" branches "that bearing boughs may live" (3. 4. 63). To save the "bearing boughs" of England was the mission of Bolingbroke; and, as men in need of health look to the good physician, so men learnt in time to look to the new King.

York   Then, as I said, the duke, great Bolingbroke . . .
          With slow but stately pace kept on his course,
          Whilst all tongues cried 'God save thee, Bolingbroke!'
Duch.   Alack, poor Richard! where rode he the whilst?
York   As in a theatre, the eyes of men
          After a well-graced actor leaves the stage,
          Are idly bent on him that enters next,
          Thinking his prattle to be tedious;

> Even so, or with much more contempt, men's eyes
> Did scowl on gentle Richard; no man cried 'God
>   save him!' (5. 2. 7)

In Pomfret Castle; troubled with his dreams (5. 5. 1); discoursing kindly of "roan Barbary" with a still loyal groom:— at the last the gentle Richard lifted his hand, not in eloquence, but action:

K. Rich. The devil take Henry of Lancaster and thee!
        Patience is stale, and I am weary of it.
                            (*Beats the keeper*)

Keep.   Help, help, help!
           Enter Exton and Servants, armed.
K. Rich. How now! what means death in this rude assault?
        Villain, thy own hand yields thy death's instrument.
        (*Snatching an axe from a servant and killing him*)
        Go thou, and fill another room in hell.
        (*He kills another. Then Exton strikes him down.*)
                            (5. 5. 102)

*   *   *

The propriety of attending the final Acts of this play may have seemed questionable to some of the audience. The deposition of an anointed king might be feared a subject unpleasing to a Queen who was later indignantly to exclaim: "I am Richard II; know ye not that?", and playgoers might naturally deem it prudent to have no part or lot in the deposition of their Sovereign. The players themselves might fear for the consequences of an unlucky indiscretion; and look to their dramatist for some play to relieve their embarrassment. Without forgoing his design to "cleanse the foul body of the infected world", in

THE LIFE AND DEATH OF KING JOHN

Shakespeare seems to have combined in a man with the

71

remedial powers of a Bolingbroke an allegiance to his Sovereign as unswerving as Elizabeth's to herself.

In this play King John is presented as the wearer of a crown which "conscience whispers" should have graced the head of his young nephew Arthur (1. 1. 40). Joined, at the instance of his mother Constance, in a holy Crusade against the usurper, France and Austria in "a resolv'd and honourable war" (2. 1. 585) have raised their banners against England; who "impatient", for his part, "of their just demands, hath put himself in arms" (2. 1. 56)

> To do offence and scath in Christendom.
>
> (2. 1. 75)

Temptation was however to assail the ears of the Crusaders. Shown "peace and fair-fac'd league" (2. 1. 417), they presently came to terms with the usurper, and, deaf to Constance's fierce cry—

> Gone to swear a peace?
> False blood to false blood join'd! gone to be
>   friends? . . .
> It cannot be, thou dost but say 'tis so (3. 1. 1)—

the confederates endeavoured to accommodate the matter with her by a disloyal subterfuge:

Philip of Brother of England, how may we content
  France This widow lady? In her right we came,
    Which we, God knows, have turn'd another way,
    To our own vantage.

K. John   We will heal up all,
    For we'll create young Arthur Duke of Bretagne
    And Earl of Richmond, and this rich fair town
    We make him lord of. (2. 1. 547)

The audience however is now to hear the words of a blunt-tongued bastard prince who, still ignorant of what he is to become (2. 1. 587) yet speaks already with the warning voice of the discerning Statesman:

> Mad world, mad kings, mad composition!
> John, to stop Arthur's title in the whole,
> Hath willingly departed with a part,
> And France, whose armour conscience buckled on,
> Whom zeal and charity brought to the field,
> As God's own soldier, rounded in the ear
> With that same purpose-changer, that sly devil . . .
> Commodity, the bias of the world—
> The world, who of itself is peised well,
> Made to run even on an even ground,
> Till this advantage, this vile-drawing bias,
> This sway of motion, this Commodity,
> Makes it take head from all indifferency,
> From all direction, purpose, course, intent:
> And this same bias, this Commodity . . .
> Clapp'd on the outward eye of fickle France,
> Hath drawn him from his own determin'd aid . . .
> To a most base and vile-concluded peace.
>
> (2. 1. 561)

This treacherous peace was however to be shown a peace no more secure than the faith of the traitors who had made it. Challenged by the voice of the Church, France is made aware that, so far from proving his faith in maintaining the peace vowed to the arch-heretic John, he has in fact disloyally broken his vow "first made to heaven",

> That is, to be the champion of our church . . .
> Therefore thy later vows against thy first
> Is in thyself rebellion to thyself;
> And better conquest never canst thou make
> Than arm thy constant and thy nobler parts
> Against these giddy loose suggestions. (3. 1. 266)

"To arms let's hie!" (3. 1. 347) became the fiery cry as much of France as of England; and the "deep-sworn faith, peace, amity, true love" (3. 1. 231) between the two was righteously ended.

The disloyalty thus renounced by France was however to reappear in a new quarter. With King John's return to England his peers found reason to forgo their vowed allegiance to him. Rumours ran rife of John's unjust imprisonment of the boy Arthur:—a little child of heaven; an innocent, like Henry the Sixth; prepared, like him, "so he were out of prison and kept sheep" to "be as merry as the day is long" (4. 1. 17); by nature gentle (2. 1. 163); loving (4. 1. 41); one to wake mercy "with his innocent prate" (4. 1. 25):—this guiltless child, men rumoured, was to die that John might reign (4. 2. 47)—

> Arthur   Alas, what need you be so boisterous-rough? . . .
> Nay, hear me, Hubert, drive these men away,
> And I will sit as quiet as a lamb;
> I will not stir, nor wince, nor speak a word,
> Nor look upon the iron angerly:
> Thrust but these men away, and I'll forgive you,
> Whatever torment you do put me to. (4. 1. 76)

Hearing presently of "a many thousand warlike French, that were embattailed and rank'd in Kent" (4. 2. 199), the English peers composed with the enemy, however compunctiously (5. 2. 11), a peace as treasonable as the previous peace concluded between the Catholic Powers and the heretic John.

> Mad world, mad kings, mad composition!

The Bastard was now, not only to denounce the evils of "commodity" (5. 1. 65), but, by inciting his "drooping" King to war (5. 1. 44; 5. 2. 128), to prescribe the remedy of the politic Statesman. England's disloyal lords were presently to become converted to the Bastard's own doctrine. So far from proving their good faith by adhering to the Frenchman, they were now to learn that they had, in fact, to their great danger, broken the earlier vow made by them to their Sovereign (5. 4. 7–61). "To arms let's hie!" became again the cry of Englishmen opposing Frenchmen, Frenchmen, Englishmen (5. 4. 60; 5. 5. 21). With the submission of John to the Pope, peace however seized the arms of war. At the Legate's urgent instance the Dauphin's Armada left the English coasts (5. 7. 89); and with the death of King John a Sovereign more likely to be followed by his subjects reigned in his stead. The loyal "faults" committed by the Bastard in the service of his rightful Master may, to his prudent fidelity, have looked no "follies" (1. 1. 262). But the champion of the English Crown, with other English lords, was now to vow himself more wholly, to no cruel King (4. 3. 126), but to a "noble prince"—

> And happily may your sweet self put on
> The lineal state and glory of the land! . . .

Prince
Henry   I have a kind soul that would give you thanks,
        And knows not how to do it, but with tears.

Bas.   O, let us pay the time but needful woe,
        Since it hath been beforehand with our griefs.
        This England never did, nor never shall,
        Lie at the proud foot of a conqueror,
        But when it first did help to wound itself.
        Now these her princes are come home again,
        Come the three corners of the world in arms,
        And we shall shock them. Nought shall make us rue,
        If England to itself do rest but true.   (5. 7. 101)

* * *

"Too little love; and too much philosophy" may perhaps have been the verdict of the playgoer on *The Life and Death of King John*. Like the Pedlar in *The Winter's Tale*, Shakespeare however had "songs for man or woman, of all sizes" (4. 4. 191), and in

THE MERCHANT OF VENICE

he seems to have "fitted his customers" by assigning the part of his 'physician' to a lady.

In *King John* Shakespeare had studied, with a national, an international malady. In *The Merchant of Venice* he selects rather one of an interracial character. Unbecoming conflicts between a Jew and a Christian are presented to the audience as infecting the prosperous City of Venice.

Shylock	Signor Antonio, many a time and oft
	In the Rialto you have rated me
	About my money and my usances ...
	You spit on me on Wednesday last;
	You spurned me such a day; another time
	You call'd me dog ...
Antonio	I am as like to call thee so again,
	To spit on thee again, to spurn thee too. (1. 3. 107)

Antonio is a man that "lends out money gratis" (1. 3. 45); a poor 'financier', but a man of substance; and to the friend of his love, his "good Bassanio", ready to unlock—

My purse, my person, my extremest means.

(1. 1. 138)

The rich merchant is hostile only to the usurious Jew who, devoted to his race (1. 3. 43), is even more so to his money—

worse poison to men's souls

than deadliest drugs (*R. and J.*, 5. 1. 80). Dearer to him than the lips of a woman or the dignities of a king, Shylock's money-bags enchant him or, in fearful dreams, forebode "some ill a-brewing towards my rest" (2. 5. 17). Shylock is not without the wit to perceive the witlessness of the Jew-baiting Christian:

> Hath not a Jew eyes? hath not a Jew hands,
> organs, dimensions, senses, affections, passions?
> fed with the same food, hurt with the same
> weapons, subject to the same diseases, healed
> by the same means, warmed and cooled by the
> same winter and summer, as a Christian is?
> (3. 1. 61)

Yet, man as Shylock is, his servant can only report himself "famished in his service" (2. 2. 113); and Jessica, his "flesh and blood", sigh only that "our house is hell" (2. 3. 2).

The conflict between Antonio and Shylock became a seed fated in time to bear the bitterest fruit. In love and in debt, Bassanio can fulfil his desires only by approaching his lover Antonio; his argosies at sea, Antonio can assist his beloved only by approaching the Jew.

Shy.   This kindness will I show,
> Go with me to a notary, seal me there
> Your single bond; and, in a merry sport,
> If you repay me not on such a day,
> In such a place, such sum or sums as are
> Express'd in the condition, let the forfeit
> Be nominated for an equal pound
> Of your fair flesh, to be cut off and taken
> In what part of your body pleaseth me.

Ant. Content, i' faith: I'll seal to such a bond,
> And say there is much kindness in the Jew.
> (1. 3. 144)

Forebodings however alike of the Jew (2. 5. 17) and the Christian (1. 1. 1) were, in a little while, to show signs of fearful fulfilment. Shylock was doomed to be robbed by his runaway daughter; Antonio, by the sea.

Shy.   A diamond gone, cost me two thousand ducats in Frankfort! . . . I would my daughter were dead at my feet and the jewels in her ear! . . . why, thou loss upon loss! . . . and no satisfaction, no revenge; nor no ill luck stirring but what lights on my shoulders. . . .

Tubal   Yes, other men have ill luck too: Antonio, as I heard in Genoa—

Shy.   What, what, what? ill luck, ill luck?

Tub.   Hath an argosy cast away, coming from Tripolis.

Shy.   I thank God, I thank God! Is't true, is't true? . . . Go, Tubal, fee me an officer . . . I will have the heart of him if he forfeit; for, were he out of Venice, I can make what merchandise I will.

(3. 1. 87)

Troubles arise at times in the world from the love of a lady. A beauty bound by her father's providential will (1. 2. 30), Portia appears on the stage as a lady destined to marry only the man who has chosen rightly in the "lottery" devised in three question-moving "chests of gold, silver and lead" (1. 2. 32). Out of love with a world of princely suitors (2. 7. 39), Portia at last fondly watches her beloved Bassanio choosing, not the glittering chests denoting Death (2. 7. 63) or Idiocy (2. 9. 54), but the dull lead whose undeceiving substance heralds the true face of Beauty—"Portia's counterfeit!" (3. 2. 115). A dream of a woman, this Heaven-elected bride is yet herself no dreamer. Philosophic (1. 2. 13); temperate (3. 2. 10, 111); sweet as the Shrew in her hour of grace (3. 2. 165), yet as forthcoming to the world as a young

Queen: in her will to befriend the stricken support of her husband Portia proceeds to play the part of the 'physician'. Pretending to retire to a monastery—there to live, like a saint,

> In prayer and contemplation (3. 4. 28),

the lady rather plots to labour like a Christian than to pray like one. Acquainted "with the cause in controversy between the Jew and Antonio" (4. 1. 154), in the disguise of a "Doctor" the girl arrives in the Court where the merciless Jew is urging his claim to the "pound of flesh", to be "by him cut off nearest the merchant's heart" (4. 1. 231).

Por.	Do you confess the bond?
Ant.	I do.
Por.	Then must the Jew be merciful.
Shy.	On what compulsion must I? tell me that.
Por.	The quality of mercy is not strain'd,

It droppeth as the gentle dew from heaven
Upon the place beneath: it is twice blest;
It blesseth him that gives, and him that takes:
'Tis mightiest in the mightiest: it becomes
The throned monarch better than his crown; . . .
It is an attribute of God himself;
And earthly power doth then show likest God's,
When mercy seasons justice . . . (4. 1. 181)

Portia's final victory in the Court gave comfort to a now gentler Antonio (4. 1. 380); and to the Jew—grown to rate revenge above riches (4. 1. 85)—such relief as man's mercy could offer him.

Por.	Art thou contented, Jew? what dost thou say?
Shy.	I am content . . .

I pray you, give me leave to go from hence;
I am not well. (4. 1. 393)

If Portia's remedy left the Jew with but a "glooming peace", to the rest she left the strength of health renewed, and, in a moonlight's artful merriments, the peace of laughing lovers rather than of staid philosophers (5. 1).

*   *   *

Without "goring his own thought" Shakespeare may in this play have thrilled a house not overcrowded with Aristotles. Like the ladies of France who had wonderfully succeeded in bringing foolish men to their senses, his Doctor Portia may, however, have seemed to him a being too remote from the work-a-day world to be at all likely to revisit it. In his plays on the reign of

KING HENRY IV

Shakespeare returns to consider with a more practical purpose the history of a man who, as the severe surgeon of a sick commonwealth, had succeeded in restoring it to some measure of health. Like many skilful surgeons Henry was, however, to learn, that, in removing some, his knife had only occasioned other, troubles in his patient. Compelled by the need of the State to "kiss" remorsefully "with greatness" (2 *H. IV*, 3. 1. 74)—

> God knows, my son,
> By what by-paths and indirect crook'd ways
> I met this crown; and I myself know well
> How troublesome it sat upon my head . . .
> > It seem'd in me
> But as an honour snatched with boisterous hand,
> And I had many living to upbraid
> My gain of it by their assistance;
> Which daily grew to quarrel and to bloodshed,
> Wounding supposed peace: all these bold fears

80

> Thou see'st with peril I have answered;
> For all my reign hath been but as a scene
> Acting that argument.   (2 *H. IV*, 4. 5. 184)

Taken for the author rather than the healer of England's "burning fever" (2 *H. IV*, 4. 1. 56); troubled to perceive—

> the body of our kingdom
> How foul it is; what rank diseases grow,
> And with what danger, near the heart of it;
> (2 *H. IV*, 3. 1. 38)

sleepless (2 *H. IV*, 3. 1. 5); forsaken (3. 1. 60); Henry could only cry as he peered into the dubious future:

> O God! that one might read the book of fate!

and see—

> how chances mock,
> And changes fill the cup of alteration
> With divers liquors!   O, if this were seen,
> The happiest youth, viewing his progress through,
> What perils past, what crosses to ensue,
> Would shut the book, and sit him down and die.
> (2 *H.* 3. 1. 45)

Peace might, through his royal exertions, "put forth her olive everywhere" (2 *H. IV*, 4. 4. 87); but to Henry Fortune never came "with both hands full" (4. 4. 103).

> The incessant care and labour of his mind
> Hath wrought the mure, that should confine it in,
> So thin that life looks through and will break out,
> (4. 4. 118)

The 'patient' proved at last too much for the 'physician'; and "his cares now ended",

> He's walk'd the way of nature;
> And to our purposes he lives no more. (5. 2. 3)

Other troubles than those recorded in Holinshed's *Chronicles* had increased the weary King's distresses. A "rude society" (1 *H. IV*, 3. 2. 14), active in the underground life of an English city, formed a cancer in the State as dangerous to its welfare as the "civil buffetings" of its brave Hotspurs and Mortimers. In this lawless society Shakespeare perceived something of that "state of nature" with which the philosopher Hobbes was presently to vex the ears of an England deprived of its lawful sovereign:

> K. Hen. O, thou wilt be a wilderness again,
>   Peopled with wolves, thy old inhabitants!
>   (2 *H. IV*, 4. 5. 137)

A multitude where "man is wolf to man" (*Leviathan*); where, rebel to the law, the "ruffian"

> will swear, drink, dance,
> Revel the night, rob, murder, and commit
> The oldest sins the newest kind of ways,
>   (2 *H. IV*, 4, 5, 125)

formed, for Shakespeare as for Hobbes, "superfluous branches" of the State which it was the duty of the Monarch and of his Lord Chief-Justice (2 *H. IV*, 5. 2. 78) to "lop away", wherever they might appear, that "bearing boughs may live".

A Bardolph, a Pistol, a lascivious Doll Tearsheet might not be unamenable to "the rusty curb of old father antic the law" (1 *H. IV*, 1. 2. 68); but there lived among this waste of "superfluous branches" one who could resist the strokes even of the Chief Justice of England (2 *H. IV*, 2. 1. 113). Though a branch less "bearing" never showed on a tree, yet this persuasive Falstaff had the wit to parry the strokes that fell at times from all quarters on him. Falstaff's body was itself a comedy: a body as humorous as Richard Crookback's had been tragic. Its immensity was the visible sign of the hungry appetites that had created it. To save the life of this body; to keep it in sack and any other of a body's amenities; was the lively aim of its owner's existence; and accordingly, like Hobbes's men of "nature" (2 *H. IV*, 3. 2. 357), he readily rated life above honour (1 *H. IV*, 5. 4. 130); cowardice above courage; and Falstaff above the world.

> By the Lord, . . . I mean not to sweat extra-
> ordinarily: if it be a hot day, and I brandish any
> thing but a bottle, I would I might never spit
> white again.   (2 *H. IV*, 1. 2. 234)

A man with a "vocation" (1 *H. IV*, 1. 2. 116) of this kind can hardly enjoy the general favour of the world. But Falstaff possessed an art well suited to assist him on the most perplexing occasions.

> A good wit will make use of any thing: I will
> turn diseases to commodity. (2 *H. IV*, 1. 2. 277)

The witty Portia might have had a pretty spar with the great creature. But the majority of men were rather bewildered into laughter than ready to maintain their more sober opinions against the stout knight's unexpected flippancies. To listen to his wit was to change the laws of England; men lost their more virtuous cares in his company; and Petruchio was not more nimble in turning Katherine's sulks into sighs than Falstaff in turning men's frowns into laughter. Intent, not on taming, but rather on cajoling, men, Falstaff could attach men to himself without alarming them; and, were he himself to be caught in their net, he had the art to slip away like an

eel, and by fictitious assertions to turn his black into white
(1 *H. IV*, 2. 4. 295). If Petruchio might confound Katherine
with the assertion that an old man was a maiden, Falstaff might
no less confound men by asserting his cowardice to be courage,
or by announcing any other improbability which, redounding
to his credit, could make men laugh without in any degree
deceiving them.

> I was as virtuously given as a gentleman need
> to be; virtuous enough; swore little; diced not
> above seven times a week; went to a bawdy-
> house not above once in a quarter—of an hour;
> paid money that I borrowed, three or four
> times; lived well, and in good compass.
>
> (1 *H. IV*, 3. 3. 16)

Men and women even injured by his generous appetites were
drawn to Falstaff as to a magnet; or as the merry may be to
the tricks of a conjurer whom they may recognize to be
somewhat less than regular in his private life.

Troubled as King Henry was by Falstaff's rude rabble, he
was more than troubled by a spirited member of it nearly
allied to himself. Falstaff's magic had induced in one greater
than a Poins or a Pistol a dream as seductive as that which the
magic of Oberon had induced in the fairy Titania (2 *H. IV*,
5. 5. 53–55).

King   God pardon thee! yet let me wonder, Harry,
 Henry   At thy affections, which do hold a wing
       Quite from the flight of all thy ancestors. . . .
       Had I so lavish of my presence been,
       So common-hackney'd in the eyes of men,
       So stale and cheap to vulgar company,
       Opinion, that did help me to the crown,
       Had still kept loyal to possession.

(1 *H. IV*, 3. 2. 29)

The Heir-Apparent was indeed sufficiently awake from the first to the strange company he kept round Falstaff:

> I know you all, and will a while uphold
> The unyoked humour of your idleness:
> Yet herein will I imitate the sun,
> Who doth permit the base contagious clouds
> To smother up his beauty from the world,
> That, when he please again to be himself,
> Being wanted, he may be more wonder'd at.
>
> (1 *H. IV*, 1, 2, 219)

No storm could disturb the commonwealth without the Prince's patriotic question: "Is it a time to jest and dally now?" (1 *H. IV*, 5. 3. 57)

> By heaven, Poins, I feel me much to blame,
> So idly to profane the precious time;
> When tempest of commotion, like the south
> Borne with black vapour, doth begin to melt,
> And drop upon our bare unarmed heads.
> Give me my sword and cloak. Falstaff, good night.
>
> (2 *H. IV*, 2. 4. 390)

Become at such moments "more himself" (1 *H. IV*, 3. 2. 93), the Prince could chide the "truant" he had been to "chivalry" (1 *H. IV*, 5. 1. 94), and clear the stain from his soul as readily as a passing shadow from his face.

So uncommon a character as the Heir Apparent's was as much an enigma to his contemporaries as were the dreaming victims of Oberon to men free from his magic. To those who saw Harry only in his dream he appeared no better than the wildest of libertines (1 *H. IV*, 5. 2. 72); to those who saw him waking he seemed to be winning the experience needful truly to "mete the lives of others" (2 *H. IV*, 4. 4. 77). In constant perplexity (*R. II*, 5. 3. 1) his royal father saw "the noble

image of his youth" (2 *H. IV*, 4. 4. 55) now in his dream
(1 *H. IV*, 3. 2. 29), and now in his waking (2 *H. IV*, 4. 5. 178).
Nor did the Prince part from his dream till his father had
parted from his life: awakened then the new King proved
that—

> England did never owe so sweet a hope
> So much misconstrued in his wantonness.
>
> (1 *H. IV*, 5. 2. 68)

Henry the Fifth could not wholly awake to 'himself' without completely abandoning his dream of Falstaff. Only as
that canker in the fair rose of the State might possibly become
a petal in it could Falstaff be received again with his followers
into the King's favour (2 *H. IV*, 5. 5. 51).

Lancaster I like this fair proceeding of the king's:

> He hath intent his wonted followers
> Shall all be very well provided for;
> But all are banish'd till their conversations
> Appear more wise and modest to the world.
>
> (2 *H. IV*, 5. 5. 103)

Henry thus became the promising successor of the weary old
physician Bolingbroke. With his coming the day had gone
when men could laugh—

> Wisdom cries out in the streets, and no man
> regards it. (1 *H. IV*, 1. 2. 99)

The sour surgeon of the commonwealth gave place to a
more smiling physician:

King   The tide of blood in me
Hen. V. Hath proudly flow'd in vanity till now:

> Now doth it turn and ebb back to the sea,
> Where it shall mingle with the state of floods,
> And flow henceforth in formal majesty . . .

No prince nor peer shall have just cause to say,
God shorten Harry's happy life one day!

(*2 H. IV*, 5. 2. 129)

*　　*　　*

Encouraged perhaps by the conversion of this promising
Prince, Shakespeare seems to have turned his thoughts for a
while to other forms of human conversion. In his play

MUCH ADO ABOUT NOTHING

Beatrice and Benedick are presented, like the unnatural
Berowne, as "whips of love" which crack in jests that leave
no scars on either, and are indeed no more than heralds of
their coming Cupid's kisses.

Ben.　　A miracle! here's our hands against our hearts.
　　　　Come, I will have thee, but, by this light, I take
　　　　thee for pity.
Bea.　　I would not deny you, but, by this good day, I
　　　　yield upon great persuasion, and partly to save
　　　　your life, for I was told you were in a con-
　　　　sumption.
Ben.　　Peace! I will stop your mouth. (*Kissing her.*)

(5. 4. 91)

This conversion of a man and a woman to their proper
amiability was coupled by Shakespeare with one of a more
significant character. In Beatrice's cousin Hero Shakespeare
presented again a "piece of life and beauty" that, beloved by
all, was by a villain's envy (1. 3; 2. 2) changed in the eye of
her duped, if too credulous, lover into a thing whose "foul-
ness" he was to "wash" wonderingly with "tears" (4. 1. 151).

Claudio　　　　　　　Would you not swear
　　　　All you that see her, that she were a maid,

87

> By these exterior shows? But she is none:
> She knows the heat of a luxurious bed;
> Her blush is guiltiness, not modesty. (4. 1. 36)

Yet, through the skill of a reverend 'physician', and the ears of listening watchmen, Claudio's folly, opened presently to timely counsels (5. 1. 288), was to be healed as surely as Benedick's. Sinning "but in mistaking" (5. 1. 269), the repentant lover was to clasp again a Beauty the lovelier in his eyes that he had seemed finally to lose it:

Friar   For it so falls out,
Francis That what we have we prize not to the worth
          Whiles we enjoy it, but being lack'd and lost,
          Why then we rack the value, then we find
          The virtue that possession would not show us
          Whiles it was ours. (4. 1. 216)

*   *   *

Much Ado About Nothing may have appeared to the play-goer a somewhat unflattering description of love's urgent business with Benedick and Beatrice. As willing to invigorate as to amuse his audience Shakespeare may however have found in certain "airy nothings" of this drama no more than a spur to his continued study of the things "cool reason contemplates". In

KING HENRY V

"the art and practic part of life" rather than unlikely fancy is exhibited as the skilled "mistress" of man's genuine "theoric" (1. 1. 51). Henry is the reason-serving 'phronimos' of Aristotle—

> Free from gross passion or of mirth or anger,
> Constant in spirit, not swerving with the blood . . .

Not working with the eye without the ear,
And but in purged judgement trusting neither.
(2. 2. 132)

"Weighing time even to the utmost grain" (2. 4. 137), he is
a man at once discrete and active—

How modest in exception, and withal,
How terrible in constant resolution! (2. 4. 34)

King as Henry was, he made no boast of his high office
(4. 1. 103), but, like his father, discovered in his duties towards his subjects responsibilities and cares unknown to
humbler mortals (4. 1. 247):

What infinite heart's-ease
Must kings neglect, that private men enjoy!
And what have kings that privates have not too,
Save ceremony, save general ceremony?
(4. 1. 253)

Conscious perhaps of Elizabeth's resentment at his daring
deposition of King Richard, Shakespeare discovers other of
the father's cares in the son:

Not to-day, O Lord,
O, not to-day, think not upon the fault
My father made in compassing the crown!
I Richard's body have interred new;
And on it have bestow'd more contrite tears
Than from it issued forced drops of blood.
(4. 1. 309)

A man as humble-minded as he was exalted (5 *Pro*. l. 20), this
"mirror of all Christian kings" (2 *Pro*. l. 6) acknowledged that
in danger we "are in God's hand" (3. 6. 178); as in success the
agents of His sovereign will and pleasure:

> O God, thy arm was here;
> And not to us, but to thy arm alone,
> Ascribe we all!   (4. 8. 111–131)

The treasons that had troubled the reign of his father could not long survive the justice of a son as severe as Henry himself in maintaining the good order of the State (2. 2):

> Touching our person seek we no revenge;
> But we our kingdom's safety must so tender,
> Whose ruin you have sought, that to her laws
> We do deliver you.   (2. 2. 174)

As little could the lawless "wolves" that had wounded the peace of his father continue to "commit the oldest sins the newest kind of ways". Nym and Bardolph met with the rigour of the law disdained by them:

> They are both hanged:

and so would Pistol be "if he durst steal any thing adventurously" (4. 4. 77). Lover of Harry's "dreaming" self, the leader of the king's "misleaders" (2 *H.IV*, 5. 5. 68) ended with his Sovereign's full awakening (4. 7. 49).

Nym   The king hath run bad humours on the knight . . .
Pist.   Nym, thou hast spoke the right;
          His heart is fracted and corroborate.   (2. 1. 127)

Not without the pity of his author—himself perhaps a little subject to his magic—Falstaff died a creature yet dearer in death than in life to his charmed followers:

Bard.   Would I were with him, wheresome'er he is,
           either in heaven or in hell!
Hostess Nay, sure, he's not in hell: he's in Arthur's
           bosom, if ever man went to Arthur's bosom. A'
           made a finer end and went away an it had been

any christom child; a' parted even just between
twelve and one, even at the turning o' the tide:
for after I saw him fumble with the sheets, and
play with flowers, and smile upon his fingers'
ends, I knew there was but one way; for his nose
was as sharp as a pen, and a' babbled of green
fields. 'How now, Sir John!' quoth I: 'what,
man! be o' good cheer.' So a' cried out, 'God,
God, God!' three or four times. . . . (2. 3. 7)

Divided in the reign of his father, King Henry's people thus
became a well-ordered society; a community like that of the
honey-bees which "by a rule in nature teach the act of order
to a peopled kingdom" (1. 2. 187).

For government, though high and low and lower,
Put into parts, doth keep in one consent,
Congreeing in a full and natural close,
Like music. (1. 2. 180)

United thus, Henry's England could engage itself in Christian
wars impossible to a distracted people (1 H. IV, 1. 1. 1–48).
Obedient to his conscience (1. 2. 96) and the will of God
(2. 2. 190), Henry led forth his swarming soldiers like armed
honey-bees to make just "boot" upon the "buds" of France
(1. 2. 194).

Now are we well resolved; and, by God's help
And yours, the noble sinews of our power,
France being ours, we'll bend it to our awe,
Or break it all to pieces. (1. 2. 222)

Dividing his "happy England into four" (1. 2. 214), Henry
presently with but a quarter of it made "all Gallia shake"
(1. 2. 216). "Consideration" which had "whipp'd the offending Adam out of him" (1. 1. 29) now whipped his soldiers'
wills against an offending France:

King   Once more unto the breach, dear friends, once more
Henry Or close the wall up with our English dead.
        In peace there's nothing so becomes a man
        As modest stillness and humility:
        But when the blast of war blows in our ears,
        Then imitate the action of the tiger;
        Stiffen the sinews, summon up the blood,
        Disguise fair nature with hard-favour'd rage.

                                      (3. 1. 1)

The tonic of Henry's valour grew more potent with the need
for it. Like the victor of Trafalgar, the victor of Agincourt
made common men "hold hard the breath and bend up every
spirit to his full height" (3. 1. 16).

        For forth he goes and visits all his host,
        Bids them good morrow with a modest smile,
        And calls them brothers, friends and countrymen . . .
        That every wretch, pining and pale before,
        Beholding him, plucks comfort from his looks.

                              (4 *Pro.* l. 32)

To the wonder of mankind this "band of brothers"

        in plain shock and even play of battle (4. 8. 114)

forced their way to a victory that, through the binding power
of the King's love for a woman, was presently to lead to a
fair peace between the war-torn kingdoms.

K. Hen. Shall Kate be my wife? . . .
Fr. King Take her, fair son, and from her blood raise up
        Issue to me; that the contending kingdoms
        Of France and England, whose very shores look pale
        With envy of each other's happiness,
        May cease their hatred, and this dear conjunction
        Plant neighbourhood and Christian-like accord
        In their sweet bosoms, that never war advance

<pre>
        His bleeding sword 'twixt England and fair France.
All   Amen!
K. Hen. Now, welcome, Kate; and bear me witness all,
        That here I kiss her as my sovereign queen.
</pre>

(5. 2. 351)

★   ★   ★

> Small time, but in that small most greatly lived
> This star of England (*Ep.* l. 5)

Bright as Henry shone, a star yet brighter was however
presently to be conceived by Shakespeare. A regent of little
England might mature into a universal "regent of the world"
(*R. II*, 2. 1. 109); and, like the sun himself, ending, with war's
dark horrors,

> every thing that seems unnatural (5. 2. 62),

possess the power to bring to the whole body of the infected
world the healing needful to it. In

JULIUS CÆSAR

Shakespeare conceived of a man whose practical wisdom had
by its sole might combined and sustained the far-flung fabric
of a universal empire. A man above "an ordinary pitch"
(1. 1. 78); who "bears the palm alone" (1. 2. 131); Cæsar was
"a Colossus" that bestrid the world (1. 2. 135): a man among
mice; a god among men (1. 2. 116). "The noblest man that
ever livèd in the tide of times" (3. 1. 256), Cæsar possessed
the distinctive character of Plato's 'Philosopher-King' and of
the rational 'Monarchos' of Aristotle:

> What touches us ourself shall be last served.

(3. 1. 8)

As resolute as he was public-minded, Cæsar looked fearlessly
upon the dangers of the world his spirit commanded:

93

What can be avoided
Whose end is purposed by the mighty gods?—
(2. 2. 26)

yet things

that threatened me
Ne'er look'd but on my back; when they shall see
The face of Caesar, they are vanished. (2. 2. 10)

As severe at times as other healers of the State, Cæsar was no
infant to be weakly wheedled out of his considered deci-
sions:

I must prevent thee, Cimber,
These couchings and these lowly courtesies
Might fire the blood of ordinary men,
And turn pre-ordinance and first decree
Into the law of children . . .
Thy brother by decree is banished:
If thou dost bend and pray and fawn for him,
I spurn thee like a cur out of my way,
Know, Cæsar doth not wrong, nor without cause
Will he be satisfied. (3. 1. 35)

With the sureness of a rational 'philosopher-king', Cæsar
could know himself, in the pursuit of his sovereign function,
to be a man as

constant as the northern star,
Of whose true-fix'd and resting quality
There is no fellow in the firmament.
The skies are painted with unnumber'd sparks; . . .
But there's but one in all doth hold his place:
So in the world; 'tis furnish'd well with men . . .
Yet in the number I do know but one
That unassailable holds on his rank,
Unshaked of motion: and that I am he,
Let me a little show it. . . . (3. 1. 60)

Uniting by such art the divers "parts" of the State, Cæsar might have been expected to compose a concord in the world "like music". But like "the music of the spheres" his was a music hard for men to follow (*M. of V.*, 5. 1. 64). The human "Olympus" (3. 1. 74) readily appeared, in the distance, another thing than he was. Worshipped by the many, there were yet persuasive detractors around him. Sore for his high flight above them, their eager envy sought to bring the eagle laughably to the ground. "When Cæsar says 'do this' it is perform'd" (1. 2. 10);—yet Cæsar was but a man! as subject as other men to human infirmities; deaf; sick; frail—as other men.

Cassius   He had a fever when he was in Spain,
        And when the fit was on him, I did mark
        How he did shake: 'tis true, this god did shake . . .
        Ay, and that tongue of his that bade the Romans
        Mark him and write his speeches in their books,
        Alas, it cried, 'Give me some drink, Titinius',
        As a sick girl. Ye gods! it doth amaze me
        A man of such a feeble temper should
        So get the start of the majestic world
        And bear the palm alone. (1. 2. 119)

Cæsar's body must be Cæsar's being; and, boasting more than it (1. 2. 116), Cæsar must be a tyrant; a usurper in a City which had not said till now

      That her wide walls encompass'd but one man.
                      (1. 2. 155)

Not to lament, but to stir men against Cæsar, the lean Cassius urged his cause of freedom:

      And why should Cæsar be a tyrant then?
      Poor man! I know he would not be a wolf

But that he sees the Romans are but sheep . .
Those that with haste will make a mighty fire
Begin it with weak straws; what trash is Rome,
What rubbish and what offal, when it serves
For the base matter to illuminate
So vile a thing as Cæsar! (1. 3. 103)

If Cassius readily persuaded men of his own kind to resent
Cæsar's pre-eminence, he worked more warily with one who,
free from envy, did not measure Cæsar's spirit by his body
(1. 2. 312–326).

Brutus   To speak truth of Cæsar,
I have not known when his affections sway'd
More than his reason. (2. 1. 19)

Brutus rather feared for Cæsar than found fault with Cæsar.
Ambition that bred tyranny in other men might breed it in
his Cæsar too.

He would be crown'd:
How that might change his nature, there's the
question . . .
But 'tis a common proof
That lowliness is young ambition's ladder,
Whereto the climber-upward turns his face;
But when he once attains the upmost round,
He then unto the ladder turns his back,
Looks in the clouds, scorning the base degrees
By which he did ascend: so Cæsar may;
Then, lest he may, prevent. (2. 1. 12)

Constant for the general good (1. 2. 85); loving "the name
of honour"; friend to high and low (1. 3. 157); yet, an imperfect judge of ordinary mortals (3. 1. 232), Brutus might
readily misjudge a man whose blood could be as little fired

by crowns and coronets as by men's "couchings and low courtesies" (3. 2. 101). Brutus permitted his fears to darken his judgement. Both in and out of love with Cæsar, like another troubled patriot (*R. II*, 2. 3. 159), he might in his dilemma have attempted to stay idly "neuter". But, once spurred by Cassius (2. 1. 61), Brutus became the leader of an enterprise alike approved and feared by him. In pity for the people (3. 1. 170), he could redden his hands in the blood of Cæsar: disdaining his adherents' fierce envy of Cæsar, his justice could cry out: "Let us be sacrificers, but not butchers" (2. 1. 166). His path once chosen, nothing could divert his trembling steps from it. Perceiving something unnatural in her Brutus, Portia might perhaps have helped to break the "hideous dream" that kept her husband sleepless (2. 1. 62).

> You've ungently, Brutus,
> Stole from my bed: and yesternight at supper
> You suddenly arose and walk'd about,
> Musing and sighing, with your arms across:
> And when I ask'd you what the matter was,
> You stared upon me with ungentle looks . . .
> It will not let you eat, nor talk, nor sleep,
> And, could it work so much upon your shape
> As it hath much prevail'd on your condition,
> I should not know you, Brutus.   (2. 1. 237)

Apprised too late however of the approaching catastrophe, Portia—with but "a woman's might"—could do no more than tremble for the fate of Brutus (2. 4.).

Heralded by portentous convulsions of Nature the death of Cæsar portended as dire convulsions of the State his life had composed and united.

Antony   A curse shall light upon the limbs of men;
Domestic fury and fierce civil strife

> Shall cumber all the parts of Italy;
> Blood and destruction shall be so in use,
> And dreadful objects so familiar,
> That mothers shall but smile when they behold
> Their infants quarter'd with the hand of war.
>
> (3. 1. 262)

Brutus did not escape the doom that darkened the now sunless world. "The noblest Roman of them all"—

Ant. His life was gentle, and the elements
So mix'd in him that Nature might stand up
And say to all the world, 'This was a man!'

(5. 5. 73)

Yet, like the ghosts of Crookback's terror, the ghost of Cæsar appeared fearfully at last to the doomed Brutus:

Bru. Ha! who comes here? . . .
Art thou some god, some angel, or some devil,
That makest my blood cold, and my hair to stare?
Speak to me what thou art. (4. 3. 275; 5. 5. 17, 50)

The past mistakes of good men whisper in man's never-forgetful conscience as reproachfully as the past sins of evil men, and in Brutus's conscience lay unburied the reproach of Cæsar's dying moments—

'Et tu, Brute?' (3. 1. 77; 5. 3. 67–71)

*　　*　　*

To lovers of liberty Brutus's mistake is as tempting as that of the critics of Plato's god-like 'Philosopher-King', and Shakespeare—aware that men may construe things

Clean from the purpose of the things themselves—
(1. 3. 35)

may have been readily induced to stage a play not less attractive and less open to misconstruction than *Julius Cæsar*. In

AS YOU LIKE IT

he presents a drama reminiscent rather of *A Midsummer Night'
Dream* than of the tragedy of Brutus. Here appear beings as
much in need as the lovers of Athens of the offices of the good
physician:—a courageous younger brother misused by an
elder brother; a usurping younger brother misusing the
daughter of an exiled elder brother. The envy which had
stalked the streets of Rome threatened danger in another city.

Oliver   My soul . . . hates nothing more than he. Yet
        he's gentle . . . of all sorts enchantingly beloved;
        and indeed so much in the heart of the world,
        and especially of my own people, who best know
        him, that I am altogether misprised: but it shall
        not be so long.   (I. I. 171)

As envious as Oliver of his brother Orlando the usurping
Duke threatens in turn his banished brother's daughter Rosalind:

Le Beau   Of late this Duke
        Hath ta'en displeasure 'gainst his gentle niece,
        Grounded upon no other argument
        But that the people praise her for her virtues,
        And pity her for her good father's sake:
        And, on my life, his malice 'gainst this lady
        Will suddenly break forth. (I. 2. 289)

A more peaceful scene however lay outside the walls of the
usurper's troubled city. In a forest as sylvan as Oberon's the
banished Duke—as weary as Henry the Sixth of striving courts
and cities—found his fortune in misfortune:

> Now, my co-mates and brothers in exile,
> Hath not old custom made this life more sweet
> Than that of painted pomp? Are not these woods
> More free from peril than the envious court? . . .
> Sweet are the uses of adversity;
> Which, like the toad, ugly and venomous,
> Wears yet a precious jewel in his head:
> And this our life exempt from public haunt
> Finds tongues in trees, books in the running brooks,
> Sermons in stones and good in every thing.
> I would not change it. (2. 1. 1)

To this wood, unknown to one another, drifted, like the
lovers of the *Midsummer Night's Dream*, Orlando and Rosalind: Orlando with an aged man whose "service sweat for
duty, not for meed" (2. 3. 58); Rosalind with her cousin Celia
—a girl that, loving Rosalind as Helena loved Hermia, could
whisper "Thou and I am one" (1. 3. 99). Like the forest of
Oberon the forest of Arden soon heard the murmur of a
lonely lover:

Orl.   O Rosalind! these trees shall be my books
     And in their barks my thoughts I'll character:
  That every eye which in this forest looks
     Shall see thy virtue witness'd every where.
  Run, run, Orlando; carve on every tree
     The fair, the chaste and unexpressive she.

                              (3. 2. 5)

As responsively the trees of the forest presently whispered the
sighs of the Rosalind eulogized in these eloquent verses:

> O coz, coz, coz, my pretty little coz, that thou
> didst know how many fathoms deep I am in
> love! But it cannot be sounded: my affection
> hath an unknown bottom, like the bay of
> Portugal. (4. 1. 209)

In this quiet woodland a more sylvan lover urged a less devoted mistress:

Silvius   Sweet Phebe, do not scorn me; do not, Phebe;
        Say that you love me not, but say not so
        In bitterness. (3. 5. 1)

The pangs of these several lovers might have been assuaged by the art of an Oberon: and luckily known to Orlando was a boy of the forest that had "since three year old" (5. 2. 66)

        been tutor'd in the rudiments
     Of many desperate studies by his uncle,
     Whom he reports to be a great magician.
                   (5. 4. 31)

An incarnate sprite from Fairyland, this young magician was destined to order the affairs of the forest with the skill of the Fairy King. The boyish-looking sprite turned out however to be something other than he appeared. Known to the laughing Celia by the name of 'Rosalind', the fair deceiver might at times be frowned on by her staider cousin:

Cel.   You have simply misused our sex in your love-
        prate: we must have your doublet and hose
        plucked over your head, and show the world
        what the bird hath done to her own nest.
                 (4. 1. 205)

Rosalind however continued so to "play the knave" (3. 2. 314) with the world as finally to prove its good physician. Having artfully pretended to Phebe to be the youth she was not (3. 5. 64), and to Orlando to be the girl that she was (3. 2. 447), she at last so contrived matters that she had only to put on a petticoat to unite true lovers together as fast as the Fairy King.

Ros.   Keep your word, O Duke, to give your daughter;

> You yours, Orlando, to receive his daughter;
> Keep your word, Phebe, that you'll marry me,
> Or else refusing me, to wed this shepherd:
> Keep your word, Silvius, that you'll marry her,
> If she refuse me; and from hence I go,
> To make these doubts all even. (5. 4. 19)

Providence completed the cure begun by Rosalind's sorceries. Converting the heart of the usurping Duke (5. 4. 167), it threw a repentant Oliver into the arms of the fair Celia (4. 3. 136; 5. 2. 35), and to the sounds of music "earthly things made even" spread mirth at last alike in heaven and earth (5. 4. 114).

Sparkling as this dream-like play must seem to lovers of Fairyland, there runs however a dark thread through it. As in *A Midsummer Night's Dream* there appears an observer who expresses Shakespeare's criticism of the follies of "the lunatic, the lover and the poet" (5. 1. 2), so in *As You Like It* appears an observer as expressive, it seems, of the poet's doubts respecting the sanity of men of all descriptions. Shakespeare could hardly have written the tragedy of *Julius Cæsar* without feeling the helplessness even of the greatest physician to

> Cleanse the foul body of the infected world
>
> (2. 7. 60)

and in melancholy "Monsieur Jacques" he appears to be covertly presenting to his audience a dramatic version of a man who, like Shakespeare himself, was apt to feel,

> a melancholy of mine own, compounded of
> many simples, extracted from many objects;
> and indeed the sundry contemplation of my
> travels, in which my often rumination wraps
> me in a most humorous sadness. (4. 1. 16)

Jacques has "gained his experience" (4. 1. 26); and, like his author at the moment of his "tiring" of the ways of mankind (*Son.* 66), is inclined to "rail against our mistress the world, and all our misery" (3. 2. 295). Lonely; understood by none; yet with the dark truth now plain to him; like Plato's "useless philosopher" Jacques can only retire from a world whose unwise wisdom his soul has rejected (2. 7. 45).

> If I heard you rightly,
> The Duke hath put on a religious life,
> And thrown into neglect the pompous court . . .
> To him will I: out of these convertites
> There is much matter to be heard and learn'd . . .
> So, to your pleasures:
> I am for other than for dancing measures.
>
> (5. 4. 186)

*   *   *

The darkness creeping into the sky above the forest of Arden may not have been observed by an audience intent rather on enjoying its growing brightness; though, if men "liked" it, they could turn their heads and see it. Intent on it as Shakespeare himself may have been, yet its threatenings were not to be discovered till, at the command of the Queen, the engaging Falstaff had been first exhibited in a new guise to his laughing admirers. In

THE MERRY WIVES OF WINDSOR

Shakespeare presents a Falstaff deprived of the magic which had sufficed to cajole those deep enough in love with "sherris-sack" (2 *H. IV*, 4. 3. 103) into becoming his well-wishers. To the merry wives there was no more magic about Falstaff than there had been to the "sober-blooded" Duke of Lancaster (2 *H. IV*, 4. 3. 92). With as little need as he to "awake" to a man

So surfeit-swell'd, so old, and so profane
(2 *H. IV*, 5. 5. 54)

they saw in Falstaff but a volume of bodily desires to make merry with. Without his former power to protect himself against his ill-wishers Falstaff became the inevitable prey of these clear-sighted ladies. Women of France had teased their lovers with a view to improving them; but these women of Windsor teased the amorous Falstaff for the simple pleasure of teasing him.

Fal.   By the Lord, a buck-basket!—ramm'd me in with foul shirts and smocks, socks, foul stockings, greasy napkins . . . Being thus cramm'd in the basket, a couple of Ford's knaves . . . were called forth by their mistress, to carry me in the name of foul clothes to Datchet-lane . . . Think of that, that am as subject to heat as butter . . . it was a miracle to 'scape suffocation. And in the height of this bath . . . to be thrown into the Thames, and cool'd, glowing hot, in that surge, like a horse-shoe; think of that; hissing hot; think of that.   (3. 5. 81)

*   *   *

Entertaining as Falstaff remained, the cloud that had threatened the pleasures of *As You Like It* may have left Shakespeare himself with but little wish to join the merry "dancing measures" of this drama; and in

TWELFTH NIGHT OR, WHAT YOU WILL

he seems to be more seriously concerned with a mysterious world ruled neither by man's wisdom nor Heaven's Providence, but rather by untutorable Time and Fate and Fortune. The men and women that now appear on his stage are alike

inclined to disallow the efficacy of the human will in the affairs
of the world. A foolish servant may be heard to cry out:
"'Tis but fortune, all is fortune" (2. 5. 22); or, making a Jove
of the blind deity, to exclaim: "Well, Jove, not I, is the doer
of this" (3. 4. 83). But more intelligent persons than he are
disposed to follow his fatalistic philosophy. With a scepticism
that touches the deepest root of the self a love-stricken girl
can sigh:

> Fate, show thy force; ourselves we do not owe;
> What is decreed must be; and be this so (1. 5. 308);

and a second girl (2. 2. 30)—maturing her thought

> What else may hap, to time I will commit—
>   (1. 2. 60)

can end more piteously:

> O time! thou must untangle this, not I;
> It is too hard a knot for me to untie! (2. 2. 39)

Men are not less fatalistic in this play than women; and, unlike
Cassius in *Julius Cæsar* (1. 2. 140), a lively youth can find the
"masters" alike of his own and of other men's days in the
"stars":

> My stars shine darkly over me; the malignancy
> of my fate might perhaps distemper yours;
> therefore I shall crave of you your leave, that
> I may bear my evils alone. (2. 1. 3)

Lucky breezes may however bring a drifting ship to port;
and the multitude—

> Not learning more than the fond eye doth teach—
>   (*M. of V.*, 2. 9. 27)

could be happily entertained by the run of a play with as
much mirth in it as a twin boy and girl could supply; to

which amusement was added, like the second subject of a frisky sonata, a diverting game with "an affection'd ass" (2. 3. 143) subject to the dangerous passion of pinnacle-climbing:

> To be Count Malvolio! . . . Having been three months married to her, sitting in my state . . . Calling my officers about me, in my branch'd velvet gown . . . And then to have the humour of state; and after a demure travel of regard . . . to ask for my kinsman Toby . . . Seven of my people, with an obedient start, make out for him: I frown the while, and perchance wind up my watch, or play with my—some rich jewel. Toby approaches; courtesies there to me,—
>
> *Sir Toby* Shall this fellow live?   (2. 5. 34)

"Golden time" might fortunately end *Twelfth Night* in a convenient sunshine (5. 1. 376). But to Shakespeare the darkness which threatened the Forest of Arden had, it seems, deepened over the darker city of Illyria. The resolute 'physician' of men makes no appearance in the scenes of this play (3. 1. 39): and—Fortune's puppets rather than its masters —its men and women want the force to say like Celia—

> Let us sit and mock the good housewife Fortune from her wheel.   (*A.Y.L.*, 1. 2. 34)

If men may at times "achieve" a greatness of their own in the world (2. 5. 139), yet man can commonly hear nothing better than that—

> Thy Fates open their hands; let thy blood and spirit embrace them.   (2. 5. 140)

Men's wills depend, it seems, on the Fates rather than the Fates on men's wills. Unfriended by these Powers, the best of Statesmen may be in the sick world of humanity as the best of physicians in an uncontrollable pestilence of Nature; and the wise man may look rather to retire from the world, like Jacques, than, like Cæsar, to meddle uselessly with it. The more the philosopher is versed in the world the more surely may he be inclined to abandon it to its fate: until the best of men may at last echo the sigh of Shakespeare's own disillusionment—

> Tired with all these, for restful death I cry . . .
>
> (*Son.* 66)

*   *   *

The storm menacing the mind of Shakespeare thundered at last in one of the most striking of his dramas. In

THE TRAGEDY OF HAMLET

Shakespeare depicts a man more nearly a true 'man' than any hitherto presented by him.

> The expectancy and rose of the fair state,
> The glass of fashion and the mould of form;
>
> (3. 1. 160)

as versed in the world's gaiety as in its business; courtier, soldier, scholar, lover; admired by the court and beloved by the people—Hamlet was, besides, by nature a 'philosopher' of no common description. "This goodly frame, the earth; this most excellent canopy, the air; this brave o'erhanging firmament; this majestical roof fretted with golden fire" (2. 2. 310) were, for this man, beauties in which his "reason" (4. 4. 38) delighted more than in the passing life of the world. "Clothed in the heavens and crowned with the stars"; like Traherne, Hamlet found, in turn, in his fellow-men the wealthy "coheirs" with himself of the philosophic treasures of reason.

> What a piece of work is a man! how noble in
> reason! how infinite in faculty! in form and
> moving how express and admirable! in action
> how like an angel! in apprehension how like a
> god! the beauty of the world! the paragon of
> animals! (2. 2. 315)

A thinker of such scope exceeds the stature even of a "regent of the world". Yet his is a mind subject to a weakness unknown to the mind of a Cæsar. The politic 'physician' of men practises his art only as he probes patiently into the ills of mankind. But one who looks to meet with beauty everywhere in the world is likely to blanch at any imperfection in it that may force itself unexpectedly on him. A sudden spot on the cheek of a Helen will, for her lover, trouble the whole face; and such a spot the unprepared Hamlet was presently to discover in the fair face of his world.

> That it should come to this!
> But two months dead! nay, not so much, not two:
> So excellent a king; that was, to this,
> Hyperion to a satyr: so loving to my mother,
> That he might not beteem the winds of heaven
> Visit her face too roughly. Heaven and earth!
> Must I remember? (1. 2. 137)

With the strange shock of his mother's sudden marriage with his uncle Hamlet's Heaven showed a stain that crept fearfully onwards over an ever blackening world.

> How weary, stale, flat and unprofitable
> Seem to me all the uses of this world!
> Fie on't! ah fie! 'tis an unweeded garden,
> That grows to seed; things rank and gross in nature
> Possess it merely. (1. 2. 133)

Ready to leave the court (1. 2. 112), Hamlet was readier still
to leave the world:

> O, that this too too solid flesh would melt,
> Thaw and resolve itself into a dew!
> Or that the Everlasting had not fix'd
> His canon 'gainst self-slaughter!   (1. 2. 129)

Melancholy; perplexed; a creature other than 'himself';
Hamlet is troubled yet further by forebodings whose hideous
import is presently to be fearfully fulfilled:

Ghost   Now, Hamlet, hear:
> 'Tis given out that, sleeping in my orchard,
> A serpent stung me . . .
>   But know, thou noble youth,
> The serpent that did sting thy father's life
> Now wears his crown.   (1. 5. 34)

Troubled before, Hamlet's Heaven grows darker yet. His
spotless Helen has become a hag; his world a thing to "vomit"
rather than to live by. The majestic beauties of Nature are
turning, for his thought, into "vapour"; and the glory of man
into a worthless "quintessence of dust" (2. 2. 304). By nature
incapable of gazing patiently on human evil, Hamlet has now
become a man who, to the eye of the true 'physician', has
broken down "the pales and forts of reason" (1. 4. 28); and
has unnaturally forfeited his proper title of "the expectancy
and rose of the fair state".

But the Ghost had still that to say to Hamlet which, discovering his peculiar weakness to him, was finally to meta-
morphose the 'man' he had been.

> If thou hast nature in thee, bear it not.   (1. 5. 81)

Called to "stir in this" (1. 5. 34), Hamlet at first is eager to

forget all that might hamper his action—"all saws of books,
all forms, all pressures past"—

> And thy commandment all alone shall live
> Within the book and volume of my brain.
>
> (1. 5. 100)

Yet—

> What to ourselves in passion we propose,
> The passion ending, doth the purpose lose.
>
> (3. 2. 204)

Hamlet's passion dying, his purpose died with it. A man of
the world like Cæsar must move the more promptly to action
the more loudly occasion summons him to it. But, with the
world his "thinking" had made for him (2. 2. 256), Hamlet
was the more inclined to loiter the more that "enterprises of
great pitch and moment" (3. 1. 86) were demanded of him.
Perceiving before him a world irretrievably ruined, Hamlet's
will breaks inevitably into pieces. He cannot deal with a
world of "dust" and "vapour". Like a musician whose
instrument lies cracked and broken before him, Hamlet can
produce none of his old music from it. Forbidden to abandon
it, he can only gaze will-lessly at it; or, vainly motioning his
hand towards it, instantly withdraw it.

> Our wills and fates do so contrary run,
> That our devices still are overthrown,
> Our thoughts are ours, their ends none of our own.
>
> (3. 2. 221)

The skilled musician can command his tune as he fingers a
true instrument, but from a disordered one can proceed, at
the fates' uncontrollable bidding, only unpredictable and
irrational noises. His will irretrievably baffled, Hamlet can
only cry:

The time is out of joint: O cursed spite,
That ever I was born to set it right! (1. 5. 189)

His "native resolution" thus

sicklied o'er with the pale cast of thought,
(3. 1. 85)

Hamlet was as little able to fulfil the Ghost's command as to close his ears to it. Imposing silence on the sharers of his secret (1. 5. 142) lest some meddling courtier should prevent the death of a King (3. 3. 8–23), yet Hamlet saved his uncle's life more surely by his doubts than any loyal tell-tale could have saved it by his words.

To be, or not to be: that is the question:
Whether 'tis nobler in the mind to suffer
The slings and arrows of outrageous fortune,
Or to take arms against a sea of troubles,
And by opposing end them. (3. 1. 56; 1. 2. 129)

In "bestial oblivion" sometimes thrusting his duty into his unconscious mind (4. 4. 40; 1. 2. 143), Hamlet wakened to it only to be troubled by a craven "thinking" that "makes cowards of us all" (3.1.83; 4. 4. 41). Sometimes seeking vainly to excuse his quiet (2. 2. 617; 3. 1. 60–88; 3.3. 74; 5. 2. 230–235); at others as vainly spurring his still loitering will (2. 2. 576–617; 4. 4. 32; 5. 2. 63); yet his purpose daily flagging, Hamlet was destined to be visited as terribly as Brutus by the unforgetting ghost of his conscience:

Do you not come your tardy son to chide,
That, lapsed in time and passion, lets go by
The important acting of your dread command?
O, say!
Ghost Do not forget: this visitation
Is but to whet thy almost blunted purpose . . .

III

Queen   Alas, how is't with you,
That you do bend your eye on vacancy
And with the incorporeal air do hold discourse?
Forth at your eyes your spirits wildly peep;
And, as the sleeping soldiers in the alarm,
Your bedded hairs, like life in excrements,
Start up and stand on end. (3. 4. 106)

Once the "king of infinite space" (2. 2. 261); imprisoned now in a Denmark that his own "thinking" had made for him; Hamlet roams the palace a being as strange to its inmates as he is to himself—

Sith nor the exterior nor the inward man
Resembles that it was. (2. 2. 6)

Severe with his erring mother (3. 2. 410; 3. 4), Hamlet moves his frightened mistress with a gaze of longing, unready to leave her. Taking "me by the wrist"—

He falls to such perusal of my face
As he would draw it. (2. 1. 90)

But, ever in love with Ophelia, Hamlet is only the more out of love with Ophelia's womanhood:

Get thee to a nunnery: why wouldst thou be a
breeder of sinners? I am myself indifferent
honest; but yet I could accuse me of such things
that it were better my mother had not borne me
. . . We are arrant knaves all; believe none of
us . . . I have heard of your paintings too,
well enough; God hath given you one face, and
you make yourselves another . . . Go to, I'll
no more on't; it hath made me mad; . . . those
that are married already, all but one, shall live;
the rest shall keep as they are. To a nunnery go.
                                           (3. 1. 122)

Assuming an actor's "antic disposition" (1. 5. 172) to cover the purpose imposed on him, Hamlet could tease a Polonius as he could have teased a cub or a kitten. A parody of the politic 'physician' of men—as foolish in deed as he was wise in conceit—"the great baby" Polonius (2. 2. 400) was "fooled" in fact by Hamlet as much as in hope Hamlet was fooled by Polonius.

Ham.	Do you see yonder cloud that's almost in shape of a camel?
Pol.	By the mass, and 'tis like a camel, indeed.
Ham.	Methinks it is like a weasel.
Pol.	It is backed like a weasel.
Ham.	Or like a whale?
Pol.	Very like a whale. (3. 2. 393)

As ironical with Rosencrantz and Guildenstern, in Horatio alone Hamlet could find the friend of his election:

> For thou hast been
> As one, in suffering all, that suffers nothing;
> A man that fortune's buffets and rewards
> Hast ta'en with equal thanks: and blest are those
> Whose blood and judgement are so well commingled
> That they are not a pipe for fortune's finger
> To sound what stop she please. (3. 2. 70)

Yet, a man inexpert in the mysteries of heaven and earth (1. 5. 166), the equable, unblanching Horatio could not fill the heart of Hamlet; and, withdrawn, at times, from men, Hamlet's "silence" would "sit drooping" (5. 1. 311).

Lonely; misconceived; as crazed to his neighbours as his neighbours were to himself; Hamlet could find in his solitude no reason for the world of irrational evil he perceived about him. Past his first wonder that a man could "smile, and smile, and be a villain" (1. 5. 108), now he wondered rather at the "one" out of "ten thousand" that could smile the smile of truth and honesty (2. 2. 178). Pondering the question whether "love lead fortune or else fortune love" (3. 2. 212–219), his thought concluded that, interpose as man (3. 2. 76) and Providence (5. 2. 10, 230) might do in the affairs of men, yet a world of evil could be dominated only by "outrageous fortune" and "the whips and scorns of time" (3. 1. 58, 70). "Lapsed in time and passion" (3, 4. 107); his will atrophied; the soul of Hamlet, as of other men, was, he perceived, a slavish instrument played on by Fortune's fingers rather than his own (3. 2. 75). "Out, out, thou strumpet, Fortune!" he could exclaim with his Players,

> All you gods
> In general synod take away her power.

But, in the world of unruled passion he perceived within him and about him, the "gods" were wanting to "break

> the spokes and fellies from her wheel,
> And bowl the round nave down the hill of heaven
> As low as to the fiends. (2. 2. 515)

It is this "outrageous fortune" rather than the will of rational 'man' which initiates the bloody end of the drama. With a random pass of his rapier Hamlet's passion has killed —he knows not whom.

Queen   O me, what hast thou done?
Ham.   Nay, I know not: is it the king?
Queen   O, what a rash and bloody deed is this! (3. 4. 25)

Rash "indiscretion" might at times appear to Hamlet an incentive to action so far superior to man's own rational fore-thought as to imply a watchful "divinity that shapes our ends" (5. 2. 6). But in killing Polonius Hamlet's rashness was so far from intimating the activity of a beneficent Providence that it was rather the irrational cause of sorrows coming, not as "single spies, but in battalions" (4. 5. 78–94). Amid scenes of murder and treachery Hamlet was to cry at last:

> "O villany! Ho! let the door be lock'd: Treachery! seek it out ... The point envenom'd too! Then, venom, to thy work. (*Stabs the King*.) ... Wretched queen, adieu! You that look pale and tremble at this chance ... Had I but time—as this fell sergeant, death, Is strict in his arrest—O, I could tell you—But let it be, Horatio, I am dead ... If thou didst ever hold me in thy heart, Absent thee from felicity a while, And in this harsh world draw thy breath in pain, To tell my story ... The rest is silence." (*Dies.*) (5. 2. 322)

Author of the deeds of erring men, Fortune is no less the author of their erring natures. The perfect 'man' offers no paradox to human reason. But evil men—as irrational as they are paradoxical—can have none but the irrational cause that men name Fate or Fortune. A single flaw of her making may bring catastrophe on her impotent victims:

> Alas, our frailty is the cause, not we!
> For such as we are made of, such we be.
> (*T.N.*, 2. 2. 30)

"Oft breaking down the pales and forts of reason", Fortune fulfils her catastrophic part in infecting, in the eyes of the world, the veritable virtues of her irresponsible victims. For—

> oft it chances in particular men,
> That for some vicious mole of nature in them,
> As, in their birth,—wherein they are not guilty,
> Since nature cannot choose his origin ...

115

Carrying, I say, the stamp of one defect,
Being nature's livery, or fortune's star,—
Their virtues else—be they as pure as grace,
As infinite as man may undergo—
Shall in the general censure take corruption
From that particular fault. . . . (1. 4. 23)

*   *   *

The chasm between the world of human 'reason' and that of man's irrational thought must remain, for a thinker of Hamlet's description, a chasm unbridgeable by human endeavour. Death might bring the philosopher to a world of "felicity" (5. 2. 358); but the world from which death took him was a world where men too faint to oppose their wills to its troubles must still draw their breath "in pain". A Hamlet however is a rare being in the world; and men of "practical wisdom" are more often to be found in it than "Kings of infinite space" (5. 2. 367). Without the design of such Statesmen Fortune's free fingers may sometimes play tunes of its own on the world; but their world is not for them an instrument so wholly impaired that it may not in some degree be tuned to play the music they wish on it. In

TROILUS AND CRESSIDA

Shakespeare proclaims once more the worth of human endeavour in a world of human chaos.

Agamemnon   Why then, you princes,
Do you with cheeks abash'd behold our works,
And call them shames? which are indeed nought else
But the protractive trials of great Jove
To find persistive constancy in men:
The fineness of which metal is not found
In fortune's love . . . (1. 3. 17–54)

It is for want of a universally recognized Ruler in the ranks of the Greeks—of a Sun among the planets—that "after seven years' siege, yet Troy walls stand" (1. 3. 1–210).

Ulysses The heavens themselves, the planets and their centre
Observe degree, priority and place ...
And therefore is the glorious planet Sol
In noble eminence enthroned and sphered
Amidst the other; whose medicinable eye
Corrects the ill aspects of planets evil,
And posts like the commandment of a king,
Sans check to good and bad. (1. 3. 85)

A man installed like Cæsar would, in the manner of the Chinese Mo-tse's ideal 'Emperor', become a Providence that

almost like the gods
Does thoughts unveil in their dumb cradles
(3. 3. 199)

and, aware of ills portending, would skilfully prevent them ere their coming. Such dethronement of "outrageous fortune" by a man

In whom the tempers and the minds of all
Should be shut up   (1. 3. 57)

might be conceived a sufficient remedy for the ills that had befallen the Greeks. To free the will of one man is, however, to free the wills of others; and Shakespeare was not unaware that even a "regent of the world" had failed wholly to "shut up" the tempers and the minds of all men. An Ajax "grown self-will'd" (1. 3. 188); an Achilles that, grown "dainty of his worth" (1. 3. 145), sulked in his tent; a Patroclus breaking "scurril jests" at wisdom (1. 3. 148):—these are men indifferent to "the still and mental parts

> That do contrive how many hands shall strike
> When fitness calls them on . . .
> Why, this hath not a finger's dignity . . .
> So that the ram that batters down the wall . . .
> They place before the hand that made the engine,
> Or those that with the fineness of their souls
> By reason guide his execution.   (1. 3. 200)

None of the heroic Greeks was a 'physician' skilled enough to deal with these self-opinionated patients. Like disordered "planets"—disobedient; egotistic; void of honour;—they perpetually maintained the "fever that keeps Troy on foot" (1. 3. 135), and made the wills of men as dangerous to the weal of the State as its worst fortunes.

Reason reigned in Troy as little as in the Greek encampments.   There, in the interest of a City imperilled by the presence of the ravished Helen, the considerate Hector could argue for a while as wisely as his wisest enemy.

> Though no man lesser fears the Greeks than I
> As far as toucheth my particular,
> Yet, dread Priam,
> There is no lady of more softer bowels . . .
> More ready to cry out 'Who knows what follows?'
> Than Hector is: the wound of peace is surety,
> Surety secure; but modest doubt is call'd
> The beacon of the wise, the tent that searches
> To the bottom of the worst. Let Helen go.
> (2. 2. 8)

A physician of man in the making; the "stay" of the State (5. 3. 60); honour's lover; merciful even to the worsted enemy (5. 3. 40); yet Hector—in want of the unshakable will of a Cæsar—weakly followed the prescriptions of his fevered patients, and bowed obediently to the "distempered blood" of the State's troublers:

> Paris and Troilus, you have both said well . . .
> not much
> Unlike young men, whom Aristotle thought
> Unfit to hear moral philosophy.
> The reasons you allege do more conduce
> To the hot passion of distemper'd blood,
> Than to make up a free determination
> 'Twixt right and wrong; for pleasure and revenge
> Have ears more deaf than adders to the voice
> Of any true decision . . .
> Hector's opinion
> Is this in way of truth: yet, ne'ertheless,
> My spritely brethren, I propend to you
> In resolution to keep Helen still;
> For 'tis a cause that hath no mean dependance
> Upon our joint and several dignities.   (2. 2. 163)

To "keep Helen still" was as certain to prolong the fevers of the war as to fail to tempt Achilles out of his tent. Two fevered armies rushed upon one another; and reason, gone from the field, left only man's folly to be mocked by the antic Thersites:

> Now they are clapper-clawing one another; I'll
> go look on.   (5. 4. 1)

The distemper of war unsettles, not alone the public, but also the private, lives of men. If Achilles repudiated his manhood in finally murdering Hector (5. 8. 10), Cressida repudiated her womanhood in finally betraying Troilus. Devout lover as Cressida appeared, Troilus might fear for her will's constancy. While "something may be done that we will not", yet

> Sometimes we are devils to ourselves,
> When we will tempt the frailty of our powers,
> Presuming on their changeful potency.   (4. 4. 96)

Tempted by the lure of warriors less simple than Troilus, Cressida, her vows undone, remorsefully confessed her traitorous amour for another:

> Troilus, farewell! one eye yet looks on thee,
> But with my heart the other eye doth see.
> Ah, poor our sex! this fault in us I find,
> The error of our eye directs our mind:
> What error leads must err: O, then conclude
> Minds sway'd by eyes are full of turpitude.
>
> (5. 2. 107)

Not through the forces of Fortune, but by man's proper turpitude reason has finally abandoned the world alike of Grecian and Trojan.

Thersites Lechery, lechery! still wars and lechery! nothing else holds fashion. A burning devil take them!

(5. 2. 195)

★ ★ ★

Yet—

as when the sun doth light a storm, (1. 1. 37)

Shakespeare was to conceive of a will which, harassed by the "frailty" of men's powers, might yet avail to deliver men from it. In

ALL'S WELL THAT ENDS WELL

the dramatist presents a girl that, "achieving" her own "goodness" (1. 1. 42), is to accomplish the impossible.

Helena Our remedies oft in ourselves do lie,
Which we ascribe to heaven: the fated sky
Gives us free scope; only doth backward pull
Our slow designs, when we ourselves are dull.

(1. 1. 213)

120

The poor daughter of a physician, through her father's secret arts Helena cures a sick king despaired of by the recognized physician.

> What I can do can do no hurt to try . . .
> He that of greatest works is finisher,
> Oft does them by the weakest minister;
> So holy writ in babes hath judgement shown,
> When judges have been babes; great floods have
>   flown
> From simple sources.   (2. 1. 134)

Helena's physical cure of a king was the prelude to her spiritual cure of a count. Loving the master of a noble family in which she was only a humble dependant, Helena lifted her eyes to a man whose scorn of her low station hid from him a love which all around perceived to be for his "reprieve" and healing (3. 4. 28).

King	She is young, wise, fair . . .
	If thou canst like this creature, as a maid,
	I can create the rest: virtue and she
	Is her own dower; honour and wealth from me.
Bertram	I cannot love her, nor will strive to do't. . . . .
Hel.	That you are well restor'd, my lord, I'm glad:
	Let the rest go.
King	My honour's at the stake, which to defeat,
	I must produce my power. Here, take her hand,
	Proud scornful boy, unworthy this good gift,
	That dost in vile misprision shackle up
	My love, and her desert . . .

Check thy contempt:

> Obey our will, which travails in thy good.
>
> (2. 3. 131)

Towards her erring husband—flying from her bed to foreign wars—Helena approved herself a woman as alert of will as she was constant in love (3. 2. 103). The Will of man was perfectly revealed in Helena. Duly restricted by the bonds of social custom, in her free action it revealed itself untrammelled by custom's unsocial conventions. Following the principle of St. Augustine, "Love, and do what you like", Helena pursued her end in a manner not wholly to be approved by a Puritan; and, declaring, with the spirit of Portia (*M. of V.*, 3. 4. 26), that she was away on a pilgrimage (3. 4. 4), sought, in fact, her beloved in the city where he was laying "wanton siege" to a chaste beauty (3. 7. 18). Men's "faults" are not always their "follies" (*K. John*, 1. 1. 262); and Helena,

> goaded with most sharp occasions,
> Which lay nice manners by, (5. 1. 14)

presently conceived a plot which,

> if it speed,
> Is wicked meaning in a lawful deed. (3. 7. 44)

Helena was to win the love of her husband in an amorous "encounter" with his beloved who,

> herself most chastely absent

from him, left Helena herself as chastely present with him (3. 7). "Reprieved" by her endeavours from "the wrath of greatest justice" (3. 4. 28), Bertram's weakness was to be as marvellously healed as the king's sickness (5. 3).

Bertram   If she, my liege, can make me know this clearly,
          I'll love her dearly, ever, ever dearly.
Hel.   If it appear not plain and prove untrue,
          Deadly divorce step between me and you!
                           (5. 3. 311)

Once "a poor unlearned virgin" (1. 3. 236), Helena has hit "where hope is coldest, and despair most fits" (2. 1. 143).

King	All yet seems well; and if it end so meet,
	The bitter past, more welcome is the sweet.
	(5. 3. 328)

*   *   *

Such a will as Helena's might be conceived to remedy, not alone the ills of lovers, but the wider-spreading evils of a human society, and in

MEASURE FOR MEASURE

Shakespeare accords to the Statesman the untrammelled powers of will of a Helena. A man "contending especially to know himself . . . a gentleman of all temperance" (3. 2. 246; 1. 3. 8): scholar, statesman and soldier (3. 2. 154); the Duke of Vienna is a philosophic "lover of the people"; one who—subject like Cæsar to their "envy, folly and mistaking" (3. 2. 149, 196; 4. 1. 60)—has as little relish as he for their "loud applause and Aves vehement" (1. 1. 71). A ruler of this nature would have seemed fitted to deal with the ills of his subjects; but mysterious as his designs appeared (1. 4. 50), he was to leave the city on a sudden like a ghost at cockcrow.

Angelo	Yet, give leave, my lord,
	That we may bring you something on the way.
Duke	My haste may not admit it. (1. 1. 61)

The Deputy appointed by the Duke to rule in his stead was a man of a kind to deal severely with the fevers of a city grown too sensual (1. 3. 50). Unstirred by the provocative arts of the wanton (2. 2. 183), Angelo was a precisian that—

doth rebate and blunt his natural edge
With profits of the mind, study and fast.
(1. 4. 60)

Set in the seat of judgement, he could fulfil his duty only as he re-instated "strict statutes and most biting laws" that, "let slip for fourteen years", were now "more mock'd than fear'd" (1. 3. 19). Striking at the lewdness of the city (1. 2. 98), he struck in turn at a man whose union with his mistress offended the letter rather than the spirit of a law long since "neglected" (1. 2. 174). Doomed to die, all hope was gone for Claudio unless his sister, by her "prosperous art" (1. 3. 189) and "grace of her fair prayer" (1. 4. 69), could soften the stern Angelo (1. 4. 75-79). "A very virtuous maid, and to be shortly of a sisterhood" (2. 2. 20), Isabella, become a "woeful suitor", was to hear only a woeful sentence:

Ang. Your brother is a forfeit of the law,
   And you but waste your words.
Isab.   Alas! alas!
   Why, all the souls that were were forfeit once;
   And He that might the vantage best have took
   Found out the remedy. How would you be,
   If He, which is the top of judgement, should
   But judge you as you are? O, think on that;
   And mercy then will breathe within your lips,
   Like man new made.
Ang.   Be you content, fair maid;
   It is the law, not I condemn your brother:
   Were he my kinsman, brother, or my son,
   It should be thus with him: he must die to-morrow.
              (2. 2. 71)

To the rigid mind of Angelo man is rather made for moral law than moral law for man. A "categorical imperative", morality is a thing to be obeyed by man without condition, mercy or remorse. "Sharp occasions" furnish no excuse to "lay it by"; and, though no harm to any may follow its breach, no unruly "exception" to it is to be willed by the good man:

Ang.   Look, what I will not, that I cannot do.
                                    (2. 2. 52)

A man like Angelo of "fast and study" might sincerely
(5. 1. 451) thrust from him a mercy which man's unphilo-
sophical mildness may venture at times to prefer to an extreme
of "justice" (2.1.4). Feel however as men may, a sufficient
surgeon of the State must sometimes use the surgeon's knife
(2. 2. 100), and Angelo might have escaped the general
censure had he continued constant to the moral principle
propounded by him. Secure however from every art of "the
strumpet", Angelo was to be shaken by the artlessness of a
saint.

Ang.   O, fie, fie, fie!
        What dost thou, or what art thou, Angelo?
        Dost thou desire her foully for those things
        That make her good? . . .
        O cunning enemy, that, to catch a saint,
        With saints dost bait thy hook! Most dangerous
        Is that temptation that doth goad us on
        To sin in loving virtue. (2. 2. 172)

Become "a devil to himself", Angelo sought to win the body
of Isabel that it might win for her the body of her brother.
That however which made Isabel a saint was also that which
must forbid the "mortal sin" required of her.

Isab.   Better it were a brother died at once,
        Than that a sister, by redeeming him,
        Should die for ever. (2. 4. 106)

In yielding her body to Bertram a Helena might outrage
custom to the greater good of both. But, in yielding herself
to Angelo, Isabella must destroy, with her own soul, the
honour of her brother.

Isab.   There is a devilish mercy in the judge,
If you'll implore it, that will free your life,
But fetter you till death.

Claud.   Perpetual durance?

Isab.   Ay, just; perpetual durance . . .

Claud.   But in what nature?

Isab.   In such a one as, you consenting to't,
Would bark your honour from that trunk you bear,
And leave you naked . . .
                              This night's the time
That I should do what I abhor to name,
Or else thou diest to-morrow.

Claud.   Thou shalt not do't.

Isab.   O, were it but my life,
I'd throw it down for your deliverance
As frankly as a pin.   (3. 1. 65)

The gain of the whole world for the loss of the soul profits man nothing; and life is death to him who wins it through another's perdition.   If, fearful at last of death (3. 1. 118), Claudio's terror cried aloud—

                    Sweet sister, let me live . . .

Isabel—as overwrought in the end as himself—could only wail at him—

                    O, fie, fie, fie!
          Thy sin's not accidental, but a trade.
          Mercy to thee would prove itself a bawd:
          'Tis best thou diest quickly.   (3. 1. 133)

Giddy; his balance lost; growing yet giddier (4. 2. 123): Angelo groaned fearfully at last—

          Alack, when once our grace we have forgot,
          Nothing goes right (4. 4. 36);

126

and learnt amid the groans of his victims that the physician
he had conceived himself to be was nothing better than a
quack who had increased his patients' fevers. In the city
Angelo was misruling had appeared however a mysterious
Friar who, watchful of these increasing disorders, made it his
business to tend and provide for them. Confessing one
(2. 3. 19); advising another (3. 1. 1); encouraging a third
(4. 2. 162); he finally contrived a general remedy for the foul
practices of the charlatan. Acceding to Angelo's lustful en-
treaties, Isabella was still to keep her honour safe:—an abandoned love of the miscreant, rather than herself, was to meet
the wanton's unknowing embraces:

Friar.   If the encounter acknowledge itself hereafter, it
           may compel him to her recompence: and here,
           by this, is your brother saved, your honour
           untainted, the poor Mariana advantaged, and
           the corrupt Deputy scaled. . . . If you think well
           to carry this as you may, the doubleness of the
           benefit defends the deceit from reproof.
                                      (3. 1. 261; 4. 1. 71)

If for the Deputy man was made for morality, for the Friar
morality was made for man. "Sharp occasions" might be
things to "lay nice manners by"; and, were all to be bettered
by their breach, no categorical imperative could stand in the
way of man's freedom. "If," the Friar might have argued, "I
do lie, and do no harm by it, though the gods hear, I hope
they'll pardon it" (Cym., 4. 2. 375; v. R. and J., 2. 3. 21;
W.T., 4. 4. 567). To the mind of the Friar Angelo's "law"
was a convenient "custom" better honoured on occasion "in
the breach than the observance" (Ham., 1. 4. 16):

           There is so great a fever on goodness, that the
           dissolution of it must cure it.

127

To restore the world, ancient customs must yield at times to new courses; and societies live rather by "truth" than by old-fashioned conventions.

> Much upon this riddle runs the wisdom of the world.   (3. 2. 235)

News of the Duke's return to the City presently reached the ears of the startled Angelo.

> His actions show much like madness; pray heaven his wisdom be not tainted! And why meet him at the gates, and redeliver our authorities there?   (4. 4. 3)

At the gates however the Duke was to complete a task which, divulged to one man only, he had been pursuing since his abandonment of the city to the care of the prim Angelo:

> To behold his sway,
> I will, as 'twere a brother of your order,
> Visit both prince and people; therefore, I prithee,
> Supply me with the habit.   (1. 3. 43)

In his friar's habit the Duke had showed—like Helena before him—the powers of a free-willed man of action: of one to whom "all difficulties are but easy when they are known" (4. 2. 221). Disdaining "fortune's" fatal fingers, like a master musician he had devised a music, new to men's ears, but true to the complete musician. In his ducal habit he was now to play a music deeper than the Friar's. A man who has ceased to measure mankind by the "law" has lost the will to "judge" mankind; and, mercy opening its doors to him, he will now be apt rather to forgive men than to punish them.

> How would you be
> If He, which is the top of judgement, should
> But judge you as you are?

128

An absentee "for fourteen years" (1. 3. 21) from a world where "corruption" had seemed to "boil and bubble till it o'errun the stew" (5. 1. 320), the Duke had now effectively accepted the world, and, passing beyond the Legalist's rejection of its evils, had also won beyond the Idealist's rejection of them. If the Duke's morality exceeded that of Angelo, his philosophy exceeded that of Hamlet. Troubled by man's wickedness, the Duke could yet look, like Heaven, patiently upon it; and, still more like Heaven, mercifully on it. Such a man will deal with the world, not only with the swift decision of a Cæsar, but with the kind "delay" that makes Heaven's gifts to men at last more precious to them.

> Duke   I will keep her ignorant of her good,
> To make her heavenly comforts of despair,
> When it is least expected. (4. 3. 113)

Looking like "power divine" upon men's "passes" (5. 1. 374), by delay (5. 1. 1–482) the Duke brings home to the guiltiest of souls the horror of its evil condition.

> Ang.   I am sorry that such sorrows I procure:
> And so deep sticks it in my penitent heart,
> That I crave death more willingly than mercy;
> 'Tis my deserving, and I do entreat it.
>   (5. 1. 479; 2. 1. 30)

But men's "deservings" are not Heaven's servings; and from the Duke, as from a mysterious incarnation of Providence, shone, at last, the sun of Heaven's forgiveness on Its children (5. 1. 483–545). "*Measure for Measure*" (5. 1. 416): "an eye for an eye". "But I say unto you, 'Love your enemies, do good to them that hate you and despitefully use you and persecute you: that ye may be the children of your Father which is in heaven.'"

CHAPTER III

INDIVIDUAL MAN

IN man's forgiving love for man Shakespeare's mature reflection has suggested the remedy which, "patiently received" by mankind, might finally "cleanse the foul body of the infected world". In the course of his reflections he has discovered physicians of differing capacities: some able, who have helped lame men to their feet; others, incompetent, who have aggravated rather than allayed their troubles. Interesting as these men and women may be for their remedial function, they are not less interesting in themselves as individual persons. An individual may be a nature as disordered as a riotous mob: and to treat of his cure be as necessary as to treat of the cure of "the infected world". Healthy men, again, may be infected by evil, as unhealthy men relieved of it; and to treat of their infection may seem a task as requisite as to treat of the infection of a healthy community.

With the improvement or deterioration of a State Shakespeare has associated the operations of a good or of an evil physician; and a man's attainment of health or his loss of it may be similarly associated with the play upon him of men good or evil. Human beings rarely raise themselves by their sole efforts; or become "devils to themselves" without the help of other men. Shakespeare has already made this truth plain to his playgoers. Without the interposition of Helena Bertram must have remained a creature "unreprieved"; and without the influence of Isabella Angelo must have remained a man whose "blood is very snow-broth". Whether with or without their intention, men are influences which, like sunshine or plague, may spread freely about them health or sickness, good or evil.

Men, however, may rise to greater heights than Bertram; or fall from greater heights than Angelo. By nature a piece of work "how infinite in faculty! in apprehension how like a god!", man can be restored to his true self only as he becomes a thing of greater significance than a social animal: a being rather cosmic than earthly; infinite rather than finite. 'Natural' as it must be for man to be 'himself', yet to reach the height of 'man' must be a thing difficult for fellows "crawling between heaven and earth" (*Ham.*, 3. 1. 130). To be precipitated from that height, however, must be as paradoxical as for a Newton to learn to discredit the truths of the mathematician. Yet—

> no perfection is so absolute,
> That some impurity doth not pollute;
>
> (*Luc.*, l. 853)

and, as in the most microscopic of men there lurk traces of an infinite faculty, so in the greatest of them may lurk some "tyrant folly".

More hardly discovered than the lurking good or evil of the social animal, these human faculties or frailties can be distinctly revealed in a man only by the intervention of persons as unusual as he is himself. By powers uncommon in the natural world the softest of leaves may be metamorphosed into things as brittle as biscuits; and by uncommon powers of human beings a man's normal nature may be metamorphosed into something no less unexpected. Like Socratic "midwives" such agents may bring to birth in a man beauties as unknown to himself as to his neighbours; or, like evil nurses, deforming passions subversive of the human reason natural and proper to him.

In

THE TRAGEDY OF OTHELLO

Shakespeare presents a man whose fall would appear as unlikely as the fall of a tower. Othello is a soldier-statesman; the acclaimed protector of his city: "whom passion could not shake; whose solid virtue the shot of accident nor dart of chance could neither graze nor pierce" (4. 1. 277):

> Another of his fathom have they none
> To lead their business. (1. 1. 153)

The hater of civil disorder, this soldier had but to appear to curb and control it:

> Why, how now, ho! from whence ariseth this?
> Are we turn'd Turks, and to ourselves do that
> Which heaven hath forbid the Ottomites?
> For Christian shame, put by this barbarous brawl:
> He that stirs next to carve for his own rage
> Holds his soul light; he dies upon his motion.
> Silence that dreadful bell: it frights the isle
> From her propriety. (2. 3. 169)

A man who would not his "unhousèd free condition put into circumscription and confine for the sea's worth" (1. 2. 26) was yet a man who found a wider freedom in a woman's love than in his Statesman's office. Not "scanting" the "serious and great business" of the State (1. 3. 268), this lover was to find in his "soul's joy"—

> content so absolute
> That not another comfort like to this
> Succeeds in unknown fate. (2. 1. 193)

The love of Othello was rather for his mistress' mind than for her body; and, "ache" as his sense might at her beauty, his love lived in her heart:

> Vouch with me, heaven, I therefore beg it not,
> To please the palate of my appetite;
> Nor to comply with heat—the young affects
> In me defunct—and proper satisfaction;
> But to be free and bounteous to her mind.
>
> (1. 3. 262)

Allured by Desdemona's 'mind' Othello was welcomed by a love as pure as his own:

> My heart's subdued
> Even to the very quality of my lord.
> I saw Othello's visage in his mind,
> And to his honours and his valiant parts
> Did I my soul and fortunes consecrate. (1. 3. 251)

Not by some magic of Oberon was "a maid so tender, fair and happy" led to prefer Othello's "sooty bosom" to the "curled darlings" of her nation (1. 2. 66). In Othello Desdemona discerned a 'man'; one who could boast "a natural and prompt alacrity" to "hardness" (1. 3. 233); a hero whose cool courage had watched unstirred the noisy cannon

> When it hath blown his ranks into the air,
> And, like the devil, from his very arm
> Puff'd his own brother. (3. 4. 134)

A wooer as "rude in speech" (1. 3, 81), for his own soldierly thought, as King Henry the Fifth (H. V., 5. 2. 149), yet Othello's words spoke in Desdemona's ear more magically than music. She marvelled at him in the midst of "most disastrous chances"; and watched him in strange worlds of "rocks, and hills whose heads touch heaven"; and with strange

> Cannibals that each other eat,
> The Anthropophagi, and men whose heads
> Do grow beneath their shoulders. (1. 3. 134)

"Beguiled" by dreaming pity Desdemona swore—

> 'twas strange, 'twas passing strange;
> 'Twas pitiful, 'twas wondrous pitiful;
> She wish'd she had not heard it, yet she wish'd
> That heaven had made her such a man.
>
> (1. 3. 160)

Othello and Desdemona were two lovers "warbling" together of "one song"; and either might have said of the other, as Celia of her Rosalind, "Thou and I am one." Yet—

> no perfection is so absolute
> That some impurity doth not pollute.

In the self-mastery of Othello lived a buried seed of mastering passion. The 'statesman' in him was not unaware of its presence in a moment of political crisis:

> Now, by heaven,
> My blood begins my safer guides to rule,
> And passion, having my best judgement collied,
> Assays to lead the way. (2. 3. 205)

Passion may turn the love of the truest of lovers to "doting"; and Othello was as aware of its uneasy presence in him as he was of the statesman's dangerous passion:

> O my sweet,
> I prattle out of fashion, and I dote
> In mine own comforts. (2. 1. 207)

Such passions might have remained no more than barren seeds in Othello; but the more dangerous of them was to be brought to birth in him by the arts of an enemy.

Iago   Ha! I like that not that.
Oth.   What dost thou say?
Iago   Nothing, my lord; or if—I know not what.
Oth.   Was not that Cassio parted from my wife?
Iago   Cassio, my lord! No, sure I cannot think it,
          That he would steal away so guilty-like,
          Seeing you coming. (3. 3. 35)

    The tempter Iago is a deliberate 'egoist': a man that, priding himself on his self-love, might have followed Richard Crookback in declaring: "Iago loves Iago: that is, I am I."

        I have looked upon the world for four times
        seven years, and since I could distinguish betwixt
        a benefit and an injury, I have never found man
        that knows how to love himself. (1. 3. 312)

A rare proficient in the egoist's calling, Iago was yet not perfect in it. He might for a moment incautiously excuse his devil's purposes (2. 3. 342). At other times he would placate his ghost of a conscience by imputing sins against himself to the victims he sinned against:

        I hate the Moor;
        And it is thought abroad that 'twixt my sheets
        He has done my office. (1. 3. 392; 2. 1. 303–316)

More surprisingly Iago once owned to a "beauty" in the life of an other that made his own "ugly" (5. 1. 19). A sufficient pupil however in the egotistical school, Iago could give a sufficiently philosophical account of its Ideal. Many a "duteous knave" "bears out his time, much like his master's ass, for nought but provender, and when he's old, cashier'd":

        Others there are
    Who, trimm'd in forms and visages of duty
    Keep yet their hearts attending on themselves,

And throwing but shows of service on their lords
Do well thrive by them, and when they have lined
their coats
Do themselves homage: these fellows have some soul,
And such a one do I profess myself. (1. 1. 49)

Men cannot throw "but shows of service on their lords" without controlling their passions, and the egoist has a Reason of his own to parry their dangers.

> If the balance of our lives had not one scale of reason to poise another of sensuality, the blood and baseness of our natures would conduct us to most preposterous conclusions: but we have reason to cool our raging motions, our carnal stings, our unbitted lusts. (1. 3. 330)

With his cool 'reason' Iago was to follow consummately the deceptive art of the egoist. "Trimm'd in forms and visages of duty", to all but the dunce Roderigo (4. 2. 184), he showed himself a man of integrity. To Othello "wise" and "honest" (4. 1. 75; 3. 3. 118, 258); to Desdemona "an honest fellow" (3. 3. 5; 4. 2. 148); to Cassio—still "kind and honest" (3. 1. 43); to his suspicious wife herself one that could grieve with grief "as if the case were his" (3. 3. 4):—thus framed to deceive, Iago appeared to all a man of his word to be surely believed. Sometimes his invention added to his subtleties (3. 3. 410; 4. 1. 94); and through him the sorceries of a handkerchief came to play a role as malignant as that of a living impostor (3. 3. 300–319). And thus, high above man's suspicion, Iago prepared and furthered a plot that, exploding the bomb of his egoism, was to wreak his revenge on Othello for preferring an other to himself (1. 1. 12):

> Cassio's a proper man: let me see now;
> To get his place, and to plume up my will

In double knavery—How, how?—Let's see:—
After some time, to abuse Othello's ear
That he is too familiar with his wife.
He hath a person and a smooth dispose
To be suspected; framed to make women false . . .
I have't. It is engender'd. Hell and night
Must bring this monstrous birth to the world's light.

(1. 3. 398)

Abusing Othello's ear Iago was not long in turning Desdemona's "virtue into pitch" (2. 3. 366). As grievously mistaken as the Roman Brutus, Othello was soon to seem as changed a being to his lover as her dear lord to Portia (3. 4. 124). But there lay in Othello that which monstrously abetted his not wholly unnatural error (3. 3. 263); in his "doting" lived a root of jealousy (3. 3. 270) that, watered by Iago, gradually overgrew the rational love of the 'man' in him.

Iago My lord, I see you're moved.
Oth.   No, not much moved.
  I do not think but Desdemona's honest.
Iago. Long live she so! and long live you to think so!
Oth. And yet, how nature erring from itself—
Iago Ay, there's the point. (3. 3. 224)

"Not poppy, nor mandragora" could presently "medicine" Othello to the "sweet sleep" he owed "yesterday".

Oth.   Ha! ha! false to me? . . .
Iago Nay, but be wise: yet we see nothing done:
  She may be honest yet. Tell me but this;
  Have you not sometimes seen a handkerchief
  Spotted with strawberries in your wife's hand?
Oth. I gave her such a one; 'twas my first gift.
Iago I know not that: but such a handkerchief—

<blockquote>

I am sure it was your wife's—did I to-day
See Cassio wipe his beard with.

Oth.   If it be that,—

Iago   If it be that, or any that was hers,
         It speaks against her with the other proofs.

Oth.   O, that the slave had forty thousand lives!
         One is too poor, too weak for my revenge.
         Now do I see 'tis true. Look here, Iago;
         All my fond love thus do I blow to heaven:
         'Tis gone. (3. 3. 330–479)

</blockquote>

"Eaten up with passion" (3. 3. 391); his wits rocking (4. 1. 36); Othello ceases to be the 'man' beloved of Desdemona. Incredulous that a handkerchief could distract an Othello, "Sure", she trembled, "there's some wonder in this handkerchief" (3. 4. 101); and, striving to excuse the miracle, her love strove rather to accuse herself than her Othello:

<blockquote>

Nay, we must think men are not gods,
Nor of them look for such observancy
As fits the bridal. Beshrew me much, Emilia,
I was, unhandsome warrior as I am,
Arraigning his unkindness with my soul;
But now I find I had suborn'd the witness,
And he's indicted falsely. (3. 4. 148)

</blockquote>

Constant in trial; finding "grace" in "checks and frowns" (4. 3. 20); forgiving evil (4. 2. 135); Desdemona's ever pure and taintless love (4. 2. 151–164) could only marvel at the causeless, ever rising fury of Othello.

Oth.   Indeed!

Des.   My lord?

Oth.   I am glad to see you mad.

Des.   Why, sweet Othello?

Oth.   Devil!   *(Striking her.)*

Des. . . . I will not stay to offend you. (*Going.*)
(4. 1. 249)

Love once present in the soul can not be finally extinguished
in it (3. 3. 90), and fading memories of love—reviving
fearfully—at times reclaimed their former sway over Othello.

Oth. O, she will sing the savageness out of a bear: of
so high and plenteous wit and invention:—
Iago She's the worse for all this.
Oth. O, a thousand thousand times; and then, of so
gentle a condition!
Iago Ay, too gentle.
Oth. Nay, that's certain: but yet the pity of it, Iago!
O Iago, the pity of it, Iago! (4. 1. 200; 4. 2. 23, 42)

Jealousy began to wane in Othello, and love to reappear in
him.

Emilia How goes it now? He looks gentler than he did.
(4. 3. 11)

But, Othello's mistake persisting in him, there remained for
him a duty not to be neglected.

Oth. Get you to bed on the instant; I will be returned
forthwith. (4. 3. 7)

Desdemona was not without love's strange forebodings.
"Prithee, to-night lay on my bed my wedding sheets"
(4. 2. 104).

Good faith, how foolish are our minds!
If I do die before thee, prithee, shroud me
In one of those same sheets. (4. 3. 23)

In her bridal bed Othello was to find his Beauty sleeping . . .

Yet I'll not shed her blood,
Nor scar that whiter skin of hers than snow

And smooth as monumental alabaster.
Yet she must die, else she'll betray more men . . .
         When I have pluck'd the rose,
I cannot give it vital growth again,
It must needs wither: I'll kiss it on the tree.
                      (*Kissing her.*)
Ah, balmy breath, that dost almost persuade
Justice to break her sword! . . .
                     I must weep,
But they are cruel tears: this sorrow's heavenly;
It strikes where it doth love . . .

Emil. (*within*) What, ho! my lord, my lord!
Oth.   Who's there? . . .
        (*Enter Emilia.*)
          . . . Alas, what cry is that?

Oth.   That! what?
Emil.   Out, and alas! that was my lady's voice . . .
Des.   A guiltless death I die.
Emil.   O, who hath done this deed?
Des.   Nobody; I myself. Farewell:
        Commend me to my kind lord: O, farewell!
                    (*Dies.*) (5. 2)

Desdemona's death was to give sudden sight to the blind:
like a lightning flash it discovered, to men's wondering horror,
Iago for the monster he was.

Oth.   Cassio did top her; ask thy husband else . . .
        Thy husband knew it all.
Emil.   My husband!
Oth.   Thy husband.
Emil.   That she was false to wedlock?
Oth.   Ay, with Cassio . . .
Emil.   My husband!
Oth.   Ay, 'twas he that told me first:
        An honest man he is, and hates the slime
        That sticks on filthy deeds.

Emil.   My husband!

Oth.   What needs this iteration, woman? I say thy
                       husband. (5. 2. 136)

Emil.   Disprove this villain, if thou be'st a man:
       He says thou told'st him that his wife was false:
       I know thou didst not, thou'rt not such a villain . . .

Iago   I told him what I thought, and told no more
       Than what he found himself was apt and true.
                        (5. 2. 172)

Oth.   O! O! O! . . . Are there no stones in heaven
       But what serve for the thunder? Precious vil-
       lain! (5. 2. 198, 235) . . . Now, how dost thou
       look now? . . . when we shall meet at compt,
       This look of thine will hurl my soul from
       heaven, And fiends will snatch at it. Cold, cold,
       my girl! . . . Blow me about in winds! roast me
       in sulphur! . . . O Desdemona! Desdemona!
       dead! (5. 2. 272) . . . I kiss'd thee ere I kill'd
       thee: no way but this, Killing myself, to die
       upon a kiss (5. 2. 358).

*   *   *

"Who", asks the broken Othello, "can control his fate?"
(5. 2. 265). A single "mole of nature" may become for man
a fate

> Oft breaking down the pales and forts of reason;

and then his "virtues else"—

> be they as pure as grace,
> As infinite as man may undergo—
> Shall in the general censure take corruption
> From that particular fault. (*Ham.*, I. 4. 23–36)

In the *Tragedy of Othello* Shakespeare has treated of nature's
mole of jealousy, and in

THE TRAGEDY OF MACBETH

he treats in turn of nature's mole of ambition.

Like Othello, Macbeth is a warrior-statesman: an acclaimed supporter of his country; "Bellona's bridegroom, lapp'd in proof" (1. 2. 54); his sovereign's "peerless kinsman" (1. 4. 58):

> As thick as hail
> Came post with post, and every one did bear
> Thy praises in his kingdom's great defence,
> And pour'd them down before him. (1. 3. 97)

Aware however as this patriot might be that "Your highness' part is to receive our duties" (1. 4. 23), the mole of Macbeth's undoing was subtly working in him. Forebodings and strange prophesyings that took the fateful form of bearded witches murmured to him, and, proclaiming his hope "Thou shalt be king hereafter" (1. 3. 50), rapt him from himself.

Banquo Good sir, why do you start, and seem to fear
        Things that do sound so fair?   (1. 3. 51)

To himself Macbeth could only argue fearfully of their real import:

> This supernatural soliciting
> Cannot be ill; cannot be good: if ill,
> Why hath it given me earnest of success . . . ?
> If good, why do I yield to that suggestion
> Whose horrid image doth unfix my hair
> And make my seated heart knock at my ribs,
> Against the use of nature?   (1. 3. 130)

The lover Othello was a man "not easily jealous" (5. 2. 345); and the patriot Macbeth one not easily ambitious. Without the "filing" of his mind (3. 1. 65), the wicked words of the witches might yet, he hoped, prove innocently effective:

> If chance will have me king, why, chance may
> crown me,
> Without my stir. (1. 3. 143)

Willing to be great, Macbeth was wanting in "the illness that should attend it"; what he willed "highly", that he willed "holily" (1. 5. 21). In the reason of a 'man', he found, with his true Self, the "vessel of his peace" (3. 1. 67); and its "eternal jewel" was not to be bartered for the throne of a beast:

> I dare do all that may become a man;
> Who dares do more is none. (1. 7. 46)

Through the wife of his bosom Macbeth however was to find the fate of his soul. Not without "the milk of human kindness": loving the babe that milked her (1. 7. 55), the father that begot her (2. 2. 13); yet Lady Macbeth was a woman who could have nodded to Emilia: "Why, who would not make her husband a villain to make him a monarch? I should venture purgatory for't." (Cf. *Oth.*, 4. 3. 75.) Apprised by Macbeth of his dark secret (1. 7. 47), his lady called her courage up and fiercely petitioned—

> That no compunctious visitings of nature
> Shake my fell purpose. (1. 5. 46)

Numbing her husband's idle will, like a momentary Iago she substituted for it one whose wind might whip him swiftly to his haven:

> He that's coming
> Must be provided for: and you shall put
> This night's great business into my dispatch.
> (1. 5. 67)

Not free from "the compunctious visitings of nature": his

sensuous thought engendering "a dagger of the mind" that "marshalled him the way that he was going" (2. 1. 42), in the dead of night, obedient to his wife, Macbeth approached the chamber of the king—

Lady M.   Hark! Peace!
    It was the owl that shriek'd, the fatal bellman
    Which gives the stern'st good-night . . .
       Enter Macbeth.
Mac. I have done the deed. Didst thou not hear a noise?
Lady M. I heard the owl scream and the crickets cry. . . .
Mac. This is a sorry sight. (*Looking at his hands.*)
Lady M. A foolish thought, to say a sorry sight.
Mac. There's one did laugh in's sleep, and one cried
            'Murder!' . . .
    One cried 'God bless us!' and 'Amen' the other . . .
    But wherefore could not I pronounce 'Amen'? . . .
Lady M.   These deeds must not be thought
    After these ways; so, it will make us mad.
Mac. Methought I heard a voice cry 'Sleep no more!' . . .
    Still it cried 'Sleep no more!' to all the house:
    'Glamis hath murder'd sleep, and therefore Cawdor
    Shall sleep no more: Macbeth shall sleep no more' . . .
Lady M.   Go get some water,
    And wash this filthy witness from your hand.
    Why did you bring these daggers from the place?
    They must lie there: go carry them, and smear
    The sleepy grooms with blood.
Mac.   I'll go no more:
    I am afraid to think what I have done;
    Look on't again I dare not.
Lady M.   Infirm of purpose!
    Give me the daggers . . .
        If he do bleed,
    I'll gild the faces of the grooms withal,
    For it must seem their guilt. (*Exit. Knocking within.*)

Mac.   Whence is that knocking? . . .
            Re-enter Lady Macbeth
Lady M. My hands are of your colour, but I shame
            To wear a heart so white . . .
                     Hark! more knocking . . .
Mac.   Wake Duncan with thy knocking! I would thou
                             couldst! (2. 2)

Dire convulsions of Nature (2. 3. 59) portended convulsions yet direr in the heart of Macbeth. "What's done is done" (3. 2. 12). But, that it may be done, yet more must needs be done. While Banquo lives "our fears stick deep" (3. 1. 49):

      We have scotch'd the snake, not kill'd it.
                             (3. 2. 13)

In the "affliction" of terrible dreams "that shake us nightly" (3. 2. 18), Macbeth prepared, alone, the deed of "dreadful note" that was at last to make him.

Lady M.   What's to be done?
Mac.   Be innocent of the knowledge, dearest chuck,
            Till thou applaud the deed. (3. 2. 44)

"Young in deed" (3. 4. 144), Banquo's murderer however was still to stand in need of his wife's resolute direction. Being done, the deed to be applauded by her paled his own cheek.

        The Ghost of Banquo enters, and sits in Macbeth's place.
Mac.   Thou canst not say I did it: never shake
            Thy gory locks at me . . .
Lady M. Sit, worthy friends: my lord is often thus,
            And hath been from his youth: pray you, keep
                          seat . . .
                       Are you a man?

Mac.   Ay, and a bold one, that dare look on that
          Which might appal the devil ...
Lady M. This is the very painting of your fear ...
                                        Shame itself!
          Why do you make such faces? When all's done,
          You look but on a stool. (3. 4. 50)

Not yet old "in deed", Macbeth looked boldly forward to
fresh deeds of horror (3.4.135–144). "Things bad begun" must
still "make strong themselves by ill" (3. 2. 55). The cries
of women; whimperings of children; began to astound a
country where "each new morn new widows howl, new
orphans cry" (4. 3. 4): a country where—no "mother" but a
"grave"—"nothing, but who knows nothing, is once seen
to smile" (4. 3. 166).

Mac.   I have supp'd full with horrors;
          Direness, familiar to my slaughterous thoughts,
          Cannot once start me. (5. 5. 13)

Fearless as the tyrant now felt in the immediate present, he
could peer still with fearful eyes into the on-coming future;
and, hearing from his witches delusive hopes of his own
destiny, in the abyss of time foresaw, with "eyeballs seared",
a line of kings of whom no one was son of his (4. 1. 48–135).
Fate fulfilled the prophesyings of the witches. "Blood-
boultered" Banquo's issue reigned in Macbeth's kingdom;
and, routed by a "moving wood", Macbeth died presently by
one "not born of woman" (5. 8. 15) ...

          I 'gin to be a-weary of the sun,
          And wish the estate o' the world were now undone.
                                        (5. 5. 49)

Tyrannous as he had been to others, Macbeth had proved a
greater tyrant to himself. Man's natural goodness must, if it

fail to revive in him, groan under the blows his unnatural wickedness rains on it.

Angus   Now does he feel
          His secret murders sticking on his hands . . .
                          now does he feel his title
          Hang loose about him, like a giant's robe
          Upon a dwarfish thief.
Menteith   Who then shall blame
          His pester'd senses to recoil and start,
          When all that is within him does condemn
          Itself for being there?   (5. 2. 16)

If Macbeth's goodness groaned with every stroke he aimed at his fellows, the goodness of an other groaned with his. Murder, which had cried out in Macbeth, was to cry out also in his partner.   The blood of her sovereign, washed readily from her hands (2. 2. 67), had irremediably reddened the memory of Lady Macbeth:

Gentle-   Look you, here she comes! . . . and, upon my
 woman   life, fast asleep . . .
Lady M.   Out, damned spot! out, I say! One: two: why,
          then 'tis time to do't . . . a soldier, and afeard?
          . . . Yet who would have thought the old man
          to have had so much blood in him? (5. 1. 22) . . .
Mac.   Wherefore was that cry?
Seyton   The queen, my lord, is dead.
Mac.   She should have died hereafter;
          There would have been a time for such a word.

To disillusioned minds time's fate however leaves man's life a thing not worth the mourning:

          To-morrow, and to-morrow, and to-morrow,
          Creeps in this petty pace from day to day,
          To the last syllable of recorded time;

147

> And all our yesterdays have lighted fools
> The way to dusty death. Out, out, brief candle!
> Life's but a walking shadow, a poor player
> That struts and frets his hour upon the stage
> And then is heard no more: it is a tale
> Told by an idiot, full of sound and fury,
> Signifying nothing. (5. 5. 15)

*   *   *

Conscious of the 'man' in them, Othello and Macbeth are as conscious of man's fall in them. Their self-reproach is to them more terrible than to common men in the degree that they have sinned more fearfully against the Self acknowledged by them. There are, however, men of an opposite character: men who, unaware of what it is to be a 'man', are as incapable as a child of perceiving errors as plain to the clear-sighted as the sun. As ignorant of self-reproach as of error, such men may nevertheless rise in time to recognise the 'man' in them; and, guilty as they may then learn to feel themselves, may finally attain the nature 'natural' to man.

In

THE TRAGEDY OF KING LEAR

appears an aged man who, to the eye of the world, shows himself the model of a father: a parent who, in the selfless love of his heart, would bestow his all on his children (1. 1). Parents may however be as possessive of their children as wives of their husbands (*T.A.*, 4. 2. 107): and, to the clearer eye, Lear's children are no other than Lear's properties. Offering what is his own to what is his, Lear gives accordingly but to himself, and, no poorer for his gifts, transfers his dignities from one full hand to the other. A man that "hath ever but slenderly known himself"; whose "best and soundest time hath been but rash" (1. 1. 296): Lear could in a moment disclaim "all his parental care" (I. I. 115) for the ungrateful child whose bold self-will had robbed him of the thing that was most his (I. I. 125); and, investing his two smiling and responsive daughters with the

> Pre-eminence and all the large effects
> That troop with majesty, (I. I. 133)

could without fear conceive his gift to be still his treasured possession:

> Only we still retain
> The name and all the additions to a king.
> (I. I. 137)

To challenge such possessive instincts is to anger a man as unaware as a child of any duty of his to control them:

Goneril Did my father strike my gentleman for chiding
of his fool?
Oswald Yes, madam.
Gon. By day and night he wrongs me; every hour
He flashes into one gross crime or other,
That sets us all at odds: I'll not endure it.
(I. 3. 1)

The gift of Lear's prerogatives to his two flattering daughters proved as fictitious as they had, from the first, conceived it to be (I. I. 308):

Gon. Idle old man,
That still would manage those authorities
That he hath given away! (I. 3. 16; I. 4. 330)

Perceiving a "most faint neglect of late"; but attributing it rather to his "jealous curiosity" than to any "purpose of un-kindness" (I. 4. 73); Lear could only stammer as he wrath-fully heard his Goneril presently censure his Fool—his servants—for "rank and not to be endurèd riots" (I. 4. 223).

Lear   Are you our daughter?

Gon.   Come, sir,
        I would you would make use of that good wisdom
        Whereof I know you are fraught, and put away
        These dispositions that of late transform you
        From what you rightly are . . .

Lear   Doth any here know me? This is not Lear . . .
        Who is it that can tell me who I am? . . .
        I would learn that; for, by the marks of sovereignty,
        knowledge and reason, I should be false persuaded I
        had daughters . . . Your name, fair gentlewoman?
                                       (1. 4. 238)

Gon.   You strike my people, and your disorder'd rabble
        Make servants of their betters.

Lear   Woe, that too late repents,— . . .

Albany   Pray, sir, be patient.

Lear (to Detested kite! thou liest.

  Gon.) My train are men of choice and rarest parts . . .
        Hear, nature, hear; dear goddess, hear!
        Suspend thy purpose, if thou didst intend
        To make this creature fruitful . . .
                    If she must teem,
        Create her child of spleen, that it may live
        And be a thwart disnatured torment to her . . .
                         that she may feel
        How sharper than a serpent's tooth it is
        To have a thankless child!   (1. 4. 277)

As amazed at the incredible sight of a servant of his set in
the stocks (2.2) by a second daughter presumed by him to be
still "kind and comfortable" (1. 4. 328)—

        What's he that hath so much thy place mistook
        To set thee here?

Kent   It is both he and she;
        Your son and daughter.

Lear	No.
Kent	Yes.
Lear	No, I say.
Kent	I say, yea . . .
Lear	They durst not do't; . . .
	Resolve me with all modest haste which way
	Thou mightst deserve, or they impose, this usage,
	Coming from us. (2. 4. 12)

A man still ignorant of defect; void of self-reproach; "So kind a father!" (1. 5. 35) to three daughters whom he had with curses severally rejected; Lear would seem a being as incapable as a possessive wife enraged with a protesting husband of attaining the selfless love of a 'man'. Men, however, learn by "suffering"; and "stepping over corpses", Hegel teaches, "is the way in which the objective spirit walks in order to reach fulfilment." The natural man must pity the pangs of a father (3. 3. 1). But to fondle an egoist is not to relieve but rather to foster the disease that torments him. Cold; unsympathetic; egotistical; yet not without grounds for their practices (1. 4. 220; 2. 2. 1–46); Goneril and Regan are now to assume more dreadful shapes:

Gon.	No, no, my lord,
	This milky gentleness and course of yours
	Though I condemn not, yet, under pardon,
	You are much more attask'd for want of wisdom
	Than praised for harmful mildness. (1. 4. 363)

The last traces of their womanhood gone out of them, the sisters' growing cruelty began insensibly to work on the heart of their father. Learning to credit the unnatural miracle of their behaviour, Lear began to feel it moving like a knife-edge in him. Self-love turning to self-pity in him; tame tears to a "noble anger" of revenges as dreadful as "the terrors of

the earth" (2. 4. 285); yet Lear could find the wish to curb
the fierceness of his passion, and, near to madness as he was,
to cry to heaven—

> You heavens, give me that patience, patience I need!
> (2. 4..274)

Useful instruments of Lear's deliverance as Goneril and
Regan proved themselves, they were yet, for all their in-
dustry, imperfect instruments. The unconscious "terrors of
the earth" (2. 4. 167) invoked by Lear on a detested daughter,
were to fall presently on his own head.

Glouces-   Alack, the night comes on, and the bleak winds
ter   Do sorely ruffle; for many miles about
       There's scarce a bush.
Reg.   O, sir, to wilful men
       The injuries that they themselves procure
       Must be their schoolmasters.   (2. 4. 303)

Cast into a night of "sheets of flame" and "bursts of horrid
thunder" (3. 2. 46)—now the World itself seemed to be
loosing its fiercest furies upon Lear. Bidding "the wind blow
the earth into the sea . . . that things might change or cease"
(3. 1. 5); Lear found in Nature's terrors the co-workers with
his daughters of an evil which yet hid a destiny of good unguessed by him.

> Here I stand, your slave,
> A poor, infirm, weak and despised old man:
> But yet I call you servile ministers,
> That have with two pernicious daughters join'd
> Your high-engender'd battles 'gainst a head
> So old and white as this. (3. 2. 19)

Subduing his old pride, Nature's furies were in secret strangely
perfecting the cruel lessons of his daughters:

No, I will be the pattern of all patience;
I will say nothing.   (3. 2. 37)

Released by patience there crept presently into the mind of Lear thoughts that mingled "reason" with his "passion" (2. 4. 237). Aware at length of his own "sinning" (3. 2. 60), he found his mind straying unwontedly into the world of the king and the philosopher:

> Let the great gods
> That keep this dreadful pother o'er our heads,
> Find out their enemies now. Tremble, thou wretch,
> That hast within thee undivulged crimes,
> Unwhipp'd of justice.   (3. 2. 49)

Like a "new-born babe" (*Mac.*, 1. 7. 21), pity presently awoke in Lear's racked heart:

> Poor naked wretches, whereso'er you are,
> That bide the pelting of this pitiless storm,
> How shall your houseless heads and unfed sides,
> Your loop'd and window'd raggedness, defend you
> From seasons such as these? O, I have ta'en
> Too little care of this! Take physic, pomp:
> Expose thyself to feel what wretches feel,
> That thou mayst shake the superflux to them
> And show the heavens more just.   (3. 4. 28)

Attaining to a knowledge of man hitherto unrevealed to him (4. 6. 97), Lear can now mock the man that "every inch a king" had lorded it over a mad world where not a man offends because all men offend (4. 6. 109, 172; v. *A.Y.L.*, 2. 7. 70). The selfless thought of the reflective 'man' begins to stir in the king; and, like a disillusioned Hamlet, he can exclaim upon the evils of a world that, a "great stage of fools" (4. 6. 187), offends the rational Ideal of 'man' now quickening in him:

> Thou rascal beadle, hold thy bloody hand!
> Why dost thou lash that whore? Strip thine own
> back;
> Thou hotly lust'st to use her in that kind
> For which thou whip'st her . . .
> Robes and furr'd gowns hide all. Plate sin with gold,
> And the strong lance of justice hurtless breaks;
> Arm it in rags, a pigmy's straw does pierce it.
> (4. 6. 164)

Out of his wits as he at times appeared, yet Lear was now a saner man than when he still controlled them.

> O, matter and impertinency mix'd!
> Reason in madness!   (4. 6. 178)

Enabled at last, with the thought of a rational 'man', to measure his once mad encounter with his daughters (1. 1), he could "by no means yield" to meet again the gaze of the youngest of them (4. 3. 42). "In his better tune", his own unkindness that "stripp'd her from his benediction" stung his mind "so venomously

> that burning shame
> Detains him from Cordelia.   (4. 3. 41)

Mankind in time may learn by suffering, yet man's salvation comes not only by means of torments. Drawing the daughter at length to the father

> Love, dear love (4. 4. 28)

was now to take its part in Lear's recovery. As kindly as Lear's Fool who in the thunder had sagely laboured to "out-jest his heart-struck injuries" (3. 1. 16), Cordelia was to begin, with love's deft fingers, the final operation upon Lear. Herself a summer; radiant; gentle; Cordelia came to him with other than the sounds of thunder.

Doctor	Be by, good madam, when we do awake him; I doubt not of his temperance.
Cor.	Very well.
Doct.	Please you, draw near. Louder the music there! . . .
Cor.	He wakes; speak to him.
Doct.	Madam, do you; 'tis fittest.
Cor.	How does my royal lord? How fares your majesty?
Lear	You do me wrong to take me out o' the grave: Thou art a soul in bliss; but I am bound Upon a wheel of fire, that mine own tears Do scald like molten lead . . . I should e'en die with pity To see another thus . . .
Cor.	O, look upon me, sir, And hold your hands in benediction o'er me. No, sir, you must not kneel.
Lear	Pray, do not mock me: I am a very foolish fond old man, Fourscore and upward, not an hour more nor less: And, to deal plainly, I fear I am not in my perfect mind . . . Do not laugh at me; For, as I am a man, I think this lady To be my child Cordelia.
Cor.	And so I am, I am. . . .
Lear	Pray you, now, forget and forgive. (4. 7. 23)

Cordelia's music however was to be interrupted. In the war waged by her with her two sisters' powers—

King Lear hath lost, he, and his daughter ta'en.
(5. 2. 6)

155

Suffering was to take the hand of Lear again. Doomed to bodily confinement, through its further operation his imprisoned spirit now found its human freedom; and, with the love, Lear won the tearless resignation of a 'man'.

> Come, let's away to prison:
> We two alone will sing like birds i' the cage:
> When thou dost ask me blessing, I'll kneel down
> And ask of thee forgiveness: so we'll live . . .
> (5. 3. 8)

But—

Edmund Come hither, captain; hark.
Take thou this note; go follow them to prison.
(5. 3. 26)

Like her two sisters Cordelia was to die a death of violence, and Lear's martyrdom to earn a more than human crown.

> *Enter Lear with Cordelia dead in his arms.*
> Howl, howl, howl, howl! O, you are men of stones: Had I your tongues and eyes, I'ld use them so That heaven's vault should crack. (5. 3. 257) . . . This feather stirs; she lives. If it be so, It is a chance which does redeem all sorrows That ever I have felt. (5. 3. 265) . . . No, no, no life! Why should a dog, a horse, a rat, have life, And thou no breath at all? Thou'lt come no more. Never, never, never, never, never! (5. 3. 305)

Yet Fate was now to make Lear "heavenly comforts of despair" where it was "least expected" (*M. for M.*, 4. 3. 113); and to his dying eyes Life showed death's shining secrets at the last in visions unrevealed to eyes less martyred:

> Pray you, undo this button: thank you, sir.

> Do you see this? Look on her, look her lips,
> Look there, look there! . . . (5. 3. 309)   (*Dies.*)

*   *   *

Othello and Macbeth are men who fall into great depths from a great height: King Lear is one who rises from great depths to heights beyond "the rack of this tough world" (5. 3. 314). Less significant examples of men of these kinds may live beside them in a single community; and in *King Lear* Shakespeare has united with the drama of a father and his daughters the attendant drama of a father and his sons. As subject to mistake as Othello, Gloucester is deceived by an illegitimate son as self-loving as Iago (1. 2); and, lured by him to seek the life of a loving son whom he loves (2. 1), he yet escapes Othello's fate, and, grown, like Lear, the manlier for the martyrdoms he endures (4. 6. 221), meets at the last a fate like Lear's:

> But his flaw'd heart,—
> Alack, too weak the conflict to support!—
> 'Twixt two extremes of passion, joy and grief,
> Burst smilingly. (5. 3. 196)

Two men of equal significance may however be conceived to rise inseparably together to their "better life"; or, falling thus together, to make, of two great sighs, a greater. Other possibilities invite the thought of the dramatist. Two men that have been great might mourn together the fate that each has brought on the other; or one that has been great and one that is to be so be conceived to play contrasting parts together on the rich stage of the world.

In the play of

ANTONY AND CLEOPATRA

appears a man who, for one particular fault—"hereditary

rather than purchased"; rather "what he cannot change than what he chooses" (1. 4. 13)—is subject, like Macbeth and Othello, to the "fate" of the great man.

> A rarer spirit never
> Did steer humanity: but you, gods, will give us
> Some faults to make us men. (5. 1. 31)

The fault the fateful gods gave Antony was to dote on a woman (1. 1. 1; 1. 2. 120). The troubled captive of this temptress, Antony had "pawned" his "experience to his present pleasure" (1. 4. 32), and, a "rebel to judgement", could not look on his charmer without losing sight of himself (1. 1. 57). Antony was lost in one whose loveliness astounded the world; who made all lesser beauties frivolous; and eyes, that had not seen her, prizeless. All things became this lady and none conquered her.

> Age cannot wither her, nor custom stale
> Her infinite variety: other women cloy
> The appetites they feed, but she makes hungry
> Where most she satisfies: for vilest things
> Become themselves in her, that the holy priests
> Bless her when she is riggish.
>
> (2. 2. 240; v. *Son*. 96)

Antony's love of this wonder was as boundless as her beauty (1. 1. 15); and, unable, like Othello, to wed love with duty (*Oth*., 1. 3. 267), in her overwhelming presence his disdain could bring destruction on an Empire:

> Let Rome in Tiber melt, and the wide arch
> Of the ranged empire fall! . . .
>
> The nobleness of life
> Is to do thus; when such a mutual pair
> And such a twain can do't. (*Embracing*.)
>
> (1. 1. 33)

Devoured by love, Antony remained however not "easily" a lover. Behind the creature of "lascivious wassails" (1. 4. 56) hid a Roman: pain-enduring; hardy; one that in war had drunk patiently "the stale of horses, and the gilded puddle which beasts would cough at" (1. 4. 61). Still "the triple pillar of the world" (1. 1. 12)—soldier and statesman—Antony was proudly conscious of the 'Roman' in him. An envoy from the city sufficed to recall him instantly to 'himself':

Ant.   Speak to me home, mince not the general tongue:
       Name Cleopatra as she is call'd in Rome.

                                (1. 2. 109–115)

The Queen herself was watchfully aware of the grave "Roman thoughts" (1. 2. 87, 120, 133), that sometimes "struck" her lover; and to keep him hers she kept him hungry (1. 3).

Cleo.   Why should you think you can be mine and true,
       Though you in swearing shake the throned gods,
       Who have been false to Fulvia? . . .
Ant.   My precious queen, forbear;
       And give true evidence to his love, which stands
       An honourable trial.
Cleo.   So Fulvia told me.
       I prithee, turn aside and weep for her;
       Then bid adieu to me, and say the tears
       Belong to Egypt. . . .
Ant.   You'll heat my blood: no more.
Cleo.   You can do better yet . . .
               But, sir, forgive me,
       Since my becomings kill me when they do not
       Eye well to you. Your honour calls you hence . . .
                    Upon your sword
       Sit laurel victory! and smooth success
       Be strew'd before your feet! (1. 3. 27)

The "strong necessity of time" commanding him (1. 3. 42), away from Cleopatra Antony resumed the manhood natural to him. In Rome again, he showed himself a Roman. A peer among his peers, he saw, once more, beyond the muds of Egypt, the World he swayed with Cæsar. Politic again; playing his part with courtesy to his foes (2. 6. 47), and with patience towards his friends (2. 2. 28); he could enjoy with them a merry feast (2. 7. 103) without thereby forgetting the controlling claims of the Empire.

Agrippa	Give me leave, Cæsar.
Cæs.	Speak, Agrippa.
Agr.	Thou hast a sister by the mother's side,
	Admired Octavia: great Mark Antony
	Is now a widower . . .
	To make you brothers and to knit your hearts
	With an unslipping knot, take Antony
	Octavia to his wife . . .
Ant.	What power is in Agrippa,
	If I would say, 'Agrippa, be it so,'
	To make this good?
Cæs.	The power of Cæsar, and
	His power unto Octavia.
Ant.	May I never
	To this good purpose, that so fairly shows,
	Dream of impediment! (2. 2. 118)

Doting merely numbed readily revives in the lover. The married Antony had little need of the mysteries of a soothsayer to bid him, like one of Macbeth's bearded witches, to "hie to Egypt again" (2. 3. 14). Night was to fall finally on Antony. In Egypt a 'Roman' no longer, he found his life again in the Rome-defying eyes of his mistress; and, forced to battle by an indignant Cæsar, lost his soldier's wit in her folly (3. 7. 29) and his courage in her cowardice (3. 10).

> Egypt, thou knew'st too well
> My heart was to thy rudder tied by the strings,
> And thou shouldst tow me after: o'er my spirit
> Thy full supremacy thou knew'st, and that
> Thy beck might from the bidding of the gods
> Command me. (3. 11. 56)

Reconciled with her, yet furious again at the sight of her hand in another's (3. 13. 85), Antony perceived in his soul's vice his reason's blindness.

> But when we in our viciousness grow hard—
> O misery on't!—the wise gods seel our eyes;
> In our own filth drop our clear judgements; make us
> Adore our errors; laugh at's while we strut
> To our confusion, (3. 13. 111)

Seeking still, after "one other gaudy night" (3. 13. 183) to break the victorious enemy, Antony's madness still grew in him.

Eno-barbus	Now he'll outstare the lightning. To be furious Is to be frighted out of fear . . .

> and I see still
> A diminution in our captain's brain
> Restores his heart. (3. 13. 195)

Foreboding evil (4. 2) among evil omens (4. 3); for the last time speaking like a king to troubled servitors (4. 2. 10); rewarding for the first time an unfaithful follower (4. 5. 12); Antony moved at last into a battle that, promising him all things, was to leave him nothing.

> All is lost;
> The foul Egyptian hath betrayed me . . .
> O this false soul of Egypt! . . .
> Whose bosom was my crownet, my chief end,

> Like a right gipsy hath at fast and loose
> Beguiled me to the very heart of loss. . . .
>
> (4. 12. 9)

But—

Dead then?

Mardian   Dead . . .

Ant.   I will o'ertake thee, Cleopatra, and
        Weep for my pardon.   (4. 14. 34)

Dead only in her fortunes, Cleopatra was to hear the last words of an Antony that, broken though he was, remained a Roman:

> The miserable change now at my end
> Lament nor sorrow at, but please your thoughts
> In feeding them with those my former fortunes
> Wherein I lived, the greatest prince o' the world,
> The noblest, and do now not basely die,
> Not cowardly put off my helmet to
> My countryman, a Roman by a Roman
> Valiantly vanquish'd. Now my spirit is going . . .
>
> (4. 15. 51)

Like Macbeth, Antony was one who had been great (3. 13. 142): but Cleopatra, like King Lear, was one who was to be so. Not without some notes of the "dark lady" who had once enthralled her creator, in youth this Queen had been of those who naturally "trade in love" (2. 5. 2). Enchanting to the eye, but troubling any reason that survived her deft glances, Cleopatra openly espoused the life of the wanton:

Ant.   I found you as a morsel cold upon
        Dead Cæsar's trencher; nay, you were a fragment
        Of Cneius Pompey's; besides what hotter hours,
        Unregister'd in vulgar fame, you have
        Luxuriously pick'd out: for I am sure,

Though you can guess what temperance should be,
You know not what it is. (3. 13. 116)

Harlots are jealous of their rivals; and Cleopatra's jealousy of
Fulvia was only topped by her fury at Octavia's rank theft of
her Antony. Striking the messenger who brought her the
pale tidings of their marriage—

What say you? Hence,
(Strikes him again.)
Horrible villain! or I'll spurn thine eyes
Like balls before me; I'll unhair thy head.
(She hales him up and down) (2. 5. 62).

Cleopatra's passions were no colder than those of other
beauties of her kind. Lovers of luxurious display (2. 2. 196);
and of life's rich banquets; things too tender to be soldiers;
like Cleopatra the "dark ladies" of the world are more regard-
ful of the wealth that comforts their bodies than of the honesty
that injures them (5. 2. 146); and, called to yield their all,
will still reserve "some lady trifles" (5. 2. 165) for themselves
"enough to purchase what they have made known" (5. 2. 148).

Yet true love sleeps, at times, in the soul, unguessed by the
many: and such a love, maturing in the mind of Cleopatra,
was to make her at the last "a lass unparallel'd" (5. 2. 319).
Proud of her person and of her men (1. 5. 29), in her Antony
there had appeared increasingly to Cleopatra something that
raised him above other men.

Charmian   The valiant Cæsar!
Cleo.   By Isis, I will give thee bloody teeth,
         If thou with Cæsar paragon again
         My man of men.
Char.   By your most gracious pardon,
         I sing but after you.
Cleo.   My salad days,
         When I was green in judgement! (1. 5. 69)

It was the Roman 'man' in Antony that Cleopatra learnt to admire together with the lusty man of flesh that smiled at her.

Cleo.   He was not sad, for he would shine on those
That make their looks by his; he was not merry,
Which seem'd to tell them his remembrance lay
In Egypt with his joy: but between both.
O heavenly mingle! Be'st thou sad or merry.
The violence of either thee becomes,
So does it no man else.   (1. 5. 55)

The Roman Antony thus became in time the wing that raised the Queen, as she had been the weight that threw the 'man' in him. Death, which at length spent his spirit, was to be for her the cordial that saved her.

My desolation does begin to make
A better life.   (5. 2. 1)

Looking for death "after the high Roman fashion" (4. 15. 87), she saw her Antony again, no woman-wooer, but the Roman "pillar of the world" (5. 2. 82–100); and, passing with her once life-loving waiting-women, met him at last in an immortal world beyond the lures of sense:

Give me my robe, put on my crown; I have
Immortal longings in me: now no more
The juice of Egypt's grape shall moist this lip . . .
                    Methinks I hear
Antony call; I see him rouse himself
To praise my noble act . . .
                    Husband, I come:
Now to that name my courage prove my title!
I am fire and air; my other elements
I give to baser life . . . (5. 2. 282)

*   *   *

164

The fortunes of a man who fell and of a woman who rose were to be indissolubly bound together again in a drama of Shakespeare. In

THE TRAGEDY OF CORIOLANUS

appears a man whose patriotic valour had been long acknowledged by a people gratefully aware

> How youngly he began to serve his country,
> How long continued. (2. 3. 244; 2. 2. 91–133)

Yet, patriot as he was (1. 9), the best of his admirers were presently to wish that Coriolanus

> had continued to his country
> As he began, and not unknit himself
> The noble knot he made. (4. 2. 30)

His virtues else "as pure as grace", through one "particular fault" of nature neither to be "helped" (1. 4. 42) nor "mended" (4. 7. 12) by him, the hero fell, like Antony, to the ground. Above the flattering praises of his countrymen (1. 9. 13, 41) Coriolanus, while not without a natural kindness (1. 9. 82), looked to have no rival beside him (2. 1. 219; 5. 6. 29–41): struggling to give his genius its freest scope, he could hence regard only with a proud contempt a mob that, competing with his power, possessed the virtue neither of soldier (1. 5. 4) nor citizen (3. 1. 21–336). That such creatures should "be still and wonder"

> When one but of my ordinance stood up
> To speak of peace or war, (3. 2. 11)

had been a lesson imparted to Coriolanus by his mother (3. 2. 7)—a lady whose lively pride lived rather in the renown of her son than in herself (1. 3).

Returned from a war in which

> All tongues speak of him, and the bleared sights
> Are spectacled to see him (2. 1. 221),

Coriolanus disclosed his irrational pride in spurning, with "a soaring insolence" (2. 1. 270), the people whose voices were to make him their consul (2. 2. 143).

Cor.　　　　　　　What must I say?—
> 'I pray, sir,'—Plague upon't! I cannot bring
> My tongue to such a pace. 'Look, sir, my wounds!
> I got them in my country's service, when
> Some certain of your brethren roar'd, and ran
> From the noise of our own drums!' (2. 3. 55)

Rejected as soon as elected (3. 1. 30); threatened with death itself by the tribune-tossed multitude (3. 1. 207); Coriolanus showed himself a man who "being once chafed" could not "be rein'd again to temperance" (3. 3. 27); and, named a "traitor" by the people (3. 1. 162; 3. 3. 66), left, with his city, his statesman's duty in it:

> Despising,
> For you, the city, thus I turn my back:
> There is a world elsewhere. (3. 3. 133)

His virtue thus "unknitted", Coriolanus' fault was to continue till it betrayed the patriot in him. The "world elsewhere" proved to be a world of enemies who, once ravaged by himself, were now, at his bidding, to ravage Rome itself. Unpardoning and revengeful (4. 5. 71); a "man" become a "dragon" (5. 4. 13); Coriolanus regretted his victory over his countrymen as little as victory over his enemies. He left his city standing because his Mother knelt for it (5. 3. 169); and, returning to the enemy "no more infected with his country's love" than when he parted from them (5. 6. 72), met his

death at the hands of a rival charmed still by the memory of
the god-like Roman he had been.

Aufidius   My rage is gone,
          And I am struck with sorrow . . .
                              Though in this city he
          Hath widow'd and unchilded many a one,
          Which to this hour bewail the injury,
          Yet he shall have a noble memory. (5. 6. 148)

If, like Antony, Coriolanus was fated to fall; like Cleopatra,
his mother was destined to rise. Professing a noble love of
her country (1. 3. 26), yet Volumnia was a mother at first
intent rather on the sovereignty, than on the service, of her
son; and, considering that "honour would become such a
person . . . was pleased to let him seek danger where he was
like to find fame" (1. 3. 10).   Not disappointed, "I have
lived", she allowed,

          To see inherited my very wishes
          And the buildings of my fancy: only
          There's one thing wanting, which I doubt not but
          Our Rome will cast upon thee. (2. 1. 214)

With the casting on him of this "one thing wanting", the
way however of the mother began to diverge from the way
of the son; in seeking to be consul Coriolanus displayed a
pride that left Volumnia frowning.

Vol.   You are too absolute;
          Though therein you can never be too noble,
          But when extremities speak. I have heard you say,
          Honour and policy, like unsever'd friends,
          I' the war do grow together: grant that, and tell me,
          In peace what each of them by the other lose,
          That they combine not there . . .

167

>   I prithee now, my son,
> Go to them, with this bonnet in thy hand . . .

Cor.   I will not do't . . .

> Lest I surcease to honour mine own truth,
> And by my body's action teach my mind
> A most inherent baseness. . . .

Vol.   Do as thou list,

> Thy valiantness was mine, thou suck'st it from me,
> But owe thy pride thyself. (3. 2. 39–131; 3. 3. 86–93)

More pliant than her son (3. 2. 52; 4. 7. 39), Volumnia—rail
as she still might at the fool tribunes (4. 2)—was finally to
mother thoughts more Roman than his. Love of her country
grew in her as it declined in him. His desertion of the city
drew her closer to it, and made her love of it at last a warring
equal with her love of him.

> Alas, how can we for our country pray,
> Whereto we are bound, together with thy victory,
> Whereto we are bound? alack, or we must lose
> The country, our dear nurse, or else thy person,
> Our comfort in the country. (5. 3. 107)

Volumnia's early lessons had taught her son the pride which
was to be his ruin: but through his pride she in turn received a
lesson that made pride for her her cherished country's ruin.
"Strains of honour",

> To imitate the graces of the gods, (5. 3. 150)

sung at last in Volumnia (5. 3. 118, 131); and, saving her
threatened country, in the place of her son Volumnia became
"the life of Rome" (5. 5. 1).

CHAPTER IV

MAN'S SALVATION

IN *Measure for Measure* Shakespeare had propounded to men
a cure for the social ills that infect them: his deeper study of
the rise and fall of individual men left the Salvation of man
a thing still subject to question. If his study had revealed to
him that

> no perfection is so absolute
> That some impurity doth not pollute,

it had also shown him that the least promising of men and
women may "come" in time "to themselves". Yet men find
"themselves", it seems, rather in an immortal world than in
the world of mankind; and learn to smile at last only as their
hearts break. To an eye still human, Tragedy seems to
darken, not alone the fate of Macbeth and Othello, but of
Cleopatra and Lear; and "general woe" (*Lear*, 5. 3. 319) to
be the lot their death leaves to the living. A further shadow
might begin to steal over the mind of the poet. His men were
rising less, and were sinking lower. With no accusing Ghost
to trouble his conscience, Coriolanus had fallen into a deeper
night than Macbeth; and, kept still mortal, Volumnia had
failed to feel the "fire and air" of Cleopatra. The human
world, for reason's rational foresight, must look a natural
Paradise. But unreason, displanting it, may seem at times
rather to have made a wild of it. Tempted to "rail against
our mistress the world" (*A.Y.L.*, 3. 2. 295), Shakespeare
might find his lips muttering like Hamlet—

> Fie on't! ah fie! 'tis an unweeded garden,
> That grows to seed; things rank and gross in nature
> Possess it merely.

A sudden storm swept across the poet's mind; and in

TIMON OF ATHENS

Shakespeare conceived of a man who, in place of his expected Paradise, perceived with curses a world strangled with every noxious weed of human lust and lovelessness.

> All is oblique;
> There's nothing level in our cursed natures
> But direct villany. Therefore be abhorr'd
> All feasts, societies and throngs of men!
> His semblable, yea, himself, Timon disdains:
> Destruction fang mankind! (4. 3. 18)

Paradise, however, is a place not to be left easily by one who has ever been in it; and Shakespeare, familiar already with the wilds of human evil, may have been only the more disposed by his last visit to them to seek again the world of beauty 'natural' to him.

> When Fortune means to men most good
> She looks upon them with a threatening eye.
> (K. John, 3. 4. 119)

Fortune's threatening eye drew Shakespeare back into a world of flowers. He now lived again, away from the turmoils of London, by the banks of the Avon, and, "the worst" returning there "to laughter" (Lear, 4. 1. 6), studied perhaps for a while no other "bursting hearts" than the brightening buds of his boyhood. Timon's world became a world as little natural to his feeling as it was to his reason. A weed-invaded garden, the world was still a garden. Men might smile in this

world as well as in an immortal one; and things of beauty
trip in it more naturally than fearful things. Shakespeare
caught sight again, among old men "reverend and venerable",
of "young men, glittering and sparkling Angels", and of
"maids, strange seraphic pieces of life and beauty".

The dramatist tunes his plays to suit his moods. If in his
tragic mood Shakespeare had staged a sin-ridden world, in his
new mood he was rather to stage a world in which sin looked
like an intruder. Into the darkness of his tragic world goodness had descended at times like a Christ; but into his new
world of light, evil, rather, was to ascend like an unwary
Titan. In this 'war in Heaven' Fate was to play a heavenly
part. No longer the tragic root in man of a "particular fault";
of a chance "mole of nature" that blasted his beauty; it was
to be, rather, through its influence upon the wills of erring
men and women, the heavenly cause of their attainment of the
beauty natural to them; of an ultimate 'salvation' not to be
rejected by them. With the spirit of a Newton confronted by
the Chance of Nature, the spirit of Shakespeare took arms
against the Chance of Fate, and, by opposing, ended it.

In three plays—

PERICLES (ACTS III–V), CYMBELINE AND THE WINTER'S TALE

the poet displays the destined victory of Heaven over the
Titans. He had not to look far for Heaven's intruding dis-
turbers. The evils that had troubled his Tragedies reappear in
these dramas: in *Pericles*, envy and the lusts of the flesh; in
Cymbeline, ambition, tyranny, imbecile lust, and a wickedness
that rivals Iago's; in *The Winter's Tale*, a fire of causeless
jealousy.

Like the usurping Duke in *As You Like It* (1. 3. 79), the
evil Dionyza envies Pericles' fair daughter for graces that

transcend the beauties of her own less noticed daughter
Philoten:

> Alack,
> That monster envy, oft the wrack
> Of earned praise, Marina's life
> Seeks to take off by treason's knife.
>
> (4 Pro., l., 11)

Elsewhere in this play lust is busy in a brothel resorted to by
gentlemen who can have never enough of a "good face",
good speech, and "excellent good clothes" (4. 2. 46). In
Cymbeline appears a shelter for all vices—a woman that, "To
work her son into the adoption of the crown" (5. 5. 37–61),
was ready smilingly to take off by poison, with a hated step-
daughter, a husband her deceits had made as tyrannical as
herself (1. 1. 125–150). The son she was working for was a
piece of amorous folly active to revenge himself on a girl who
preferred an "eagle" to the puny "puttock" he appeared to
her (1. 1. 139).

Cloten   I love and hate her: for she's fair and royal,
    And that she hath all courtly parts more exquisite
    Than lady, ladies, woman . . .
         I love her therefore; but
    Disdaining me and throwing favours on
    The low Posthumus slanders so her judgement
    That what's else rare is choked; and in that point
    I will conclude to hate her, nay, indeed,
    To be revenged upon her. (3. 5. 70)

In this play, again, appears an egoist as devoted as Iago and
Edmund to the injury of other men; a man who, sceptical of
women's virtue, wagers to "assail" successfully the lovely
partner of the loyal Posthumus (1. 4. 136–182). Watching,
amazed, her sleeping beauty—

> If she be furnish'd with a mind so rare,
> She is alone the Arabian bird, and I
> Have lost the wager. Boldness be my friend!
> Arm me, audacity, from head to foot!
>
> (1. 6. 16)

Not less audacious than Iachimo, a Titan of Jealousy dreams, in *The Winter's Tale*, to burn, with the baby of a day (2. 3. 134), a wife as pure as Grace. "She—

> I can hook to me: say that she were gone,
> Given to the fire, a moiety of my rest
> Might come to me again. (2. 3. 6)

Ready for battle as these Titans were, yet their audacity was to remain unrewarded: neither soul nor body of their enemies was fated to fall victim to them (*Per.*, 5. 3. 89). A "seraphic piece of life and beauty", the daughter of Pericles suffered no hurt from their onset. Born into a Timon-like world whose troubled waters buried her mother (3. 1), Marina grew up a creature that, skilled to "wound the cambric" (4 *Pro.*, l. 23), yet never did ill turn

> To any living creature: believe me, la,
> I never kill'd a mouse, nor hurt a fly:
> I trod upon a worm against my will,
> But I wept for it. (4. 1. 76)

Escaping the dart of Dionyza, Marina was to suffer no wound in the brothels of Mitylene. "An honest woman—or not a woman" (4. 2. 82) was the philosophy of Marina as it had been the philosophy of Desdemona (*Oth.*, 4. 3. 78):

> If fires be hot, knives sharp, or waters deep,
> Untied I still my virgin knot will keep.
> Diana, aid my purpose! (4. 2. 144)

The brothel's doors soon opened to Marina; and, able, like

Desdemona, to "sing, weave, sew, and dance" (4. 6. 178), in an "honest house" she presently found pupils "of noble race" to "pour their bounty on her" (5 Pro. l. 9).

As fiercely assailed as Marina, another "seraphic piece of life and beauty" remained unwounded in a more severely contested part of the field. Engaged with ambition, tyranny, lust and treachery, Imogen yet remained 'herself': a woman as faultless in mind as in body. Believing her husband to have betrayed her love for a wanton, she might momentarily disbelieve a faithful attendant whose wisdom counselled her:

Pisanio   It cannot be
But that my master is abused; some villain,
Ay, and singular in his art, hath done you both
This cursed injury.
Imo.   Some Roman courtezan. (3. 4. 122)

Yet Imogen continued constant; and, clinging to her lover, was to hear at last words that healed her troubles:

Posthumus   Hang there like fruit, my soul,
Till the tree die! (5. 5. 263)

More wounded in the conflict than herself, Posthumus—than whom

a nobler sir ne'er lived
'Twixt sky and ground (5. 5. 145)--

met in Iachimo with a Titan as dangerous as Iago had been to Othello; and, in error like the Moor, lost for a while the beauty proper to him in a fury matching Othello's (2. 5; 3. 4). With his error's discovery crying like Othello on Desdemona—

O Imogen,
My queen, my life, my wife! O Imogen!
(5. 5. 225)

yet Posthumus was to live and love again. Not dying like
Othello "upon a kiss", he returned to 'himself' in finding a
yet living Imogen by means of one:

Imo.   Why did you throw your wedded lady from you?
         Think that you are upon a rock, and now
         Throw me again.   (*Embracing him.*) (5. 5. 261)

Beset as fiercely as Imogen, a maturer Beauty found her
virtue challenged in another part of the field. Heart-struck,
yet invulnerable as Marina, the Queen of Leontes remained
as unhurt by his cry "She's an adulteress" as by the hook
with which he thought to heave her firewards:

Hermione   Should a villain say so,
         The most replenish'd villain in the world,
         He were as much more villain: you, my lord,
         Do but mistake. (2. 1. 78)

Hermione remained 'herself' (3. 2. 1–124); and, more fortunate than Desdemona, with the help of her Paulina, was to
tell at last how she had "stolen from the dead" (5. 3. 115, 153).

The Titans proved to be, in the end, as unwary as they were
unsuccessful. The justice of "the gods", or their own despair,
might be the end of some of them (*Per.* 5. 3. 96; *Cym.*,
4. 2. 113; 5. 5. 30); but through the influence of Heaven's
ministers, more were to die to their own evil, and, through
a salvation not to be rejected by them, to attain at last the
beauty natural to 'man'. A Dionyza, a Cloten, a wicked
Queen might lie dead on the battlefield; but others, rising,
were destined to look at last not unlike their conquerors.

Weak as she seemed, Marina, her rueful captors confessed,
was "born " to "undo" them (4. 6. 145).

         She makes our profession as it were to stink afore
         the face of the gods. (4. 6. 132)

175

Gentlemen "out of the road of rutting" left the pandar's brothel with the idea of doing "any thing that is virtuous" (4. 5. 8); and the Governor of Mitylene in Marina's pure presence (4. 6) became a "noble" Lysimachus, worthy to win his young conqueror's hand (5. 1. 262).

Fraud was to fare in this world no better than lust. The dart aimed at love by Iachimo was in the end to hit his own conscience:

> I am glad to be constrain'd to utter that
> Which torments me to conceal . . .
>   That paragon, thy daughter,
> For whom my heart drops blood and my false
>   spirits
> Quail to remember—Give me leave; I faint . . .
>   (5. 5. 141)

The sinner's fainting preluded a new birth in him. Kneeling penitently before the injured Posthumus, he was to be made at last the 'man' he had not been.

Post.   Kneel not to me:
> The power that I have on you is to spare you;
> The malice towards you to forgive you: live,
> And deal with others better. (5. 5. 417)

Leontes was to share the fate of the other Titans. As little able as they to withstand the Powers of the world around him, he yielded quickly to the voice of the divine Apollo: "Hermione is chaste . . . Leontes a jealous tyrant" (3. 2. 133). "Touched to the noble heart" (3. 2. 222), he became a lover of unending repentance (5. 1. 1). Like the suffering Lear, Leontes could scarcely pardon himself; till, happier than Lear, he met again in the mortal world about him the love he had despaired of.

Leon.   O, she's warm!
      If this be magic, let it be an art
      Lawful as eating.
Pol.   She embraces him.
Cam.   She hangs about his neck . . . (5. 3. 109)

Timon had met with an inhuman world where "feasts,
societies and throngs of men" were to be "abhorr'd". But,
in the human world which Shakespeare's thought had substituted for it, love found its natural home and resting-place.
If the beings native to this world were strong to clear its
beauty of invading evils, they were as apt to charm away its
bodily ailments. Wickedness might end the life of an innocent
(*W. T.*, 3. 2. 145); but love still had the better of the conflict.
A father dumb for grief could be readily relieved by a Marina.

      She, questionless, with her sweet harmony
      And other chosen attractions, would allure,
      And make a battery through his deafen'd parts,
      Which now are midway stopp'd.   (5. 1. 45)

Grave men of reverend looks (*W.T.*, 3. 1. 5) were as strong as
youth to heal, with the minds, the bodies of their patients;
and, like immortal gods (*Per.*, 3. 2. 30) "pour'd forth" their
charity till "hundreds" called themselves their "creatures"
(*Per.*, 3. 2. 44). Brothers unknown to her comforted the
sufferings of Imogen; and, when she seemed to die, still conceived of "wench-like" comforts for her resting-place
(*Cym.*, 4. 2. 218–231).

                With fairest flowers,
      Whilst summer lasts, and I live here, Fidele,
      I'll sweeten thy sad grave: thou shalt not lack
      The flower that's like thy face, pale primrose, nor
      The azured harebell, like thy veins.

177

Flowery places were more to the liking of these unspoiled natures than the artificial courts of princes; and "low roofs" better instructors than palaces of the way "to adore the heavens" (*Cym.*, 3. 3. 2).

Belarius　　　　　　　　To apprehend thus,
Draws us a profit from all things we see;
And often, to our comfort, shall we find
The sharded beetle in a safer hold
Than is the full-wing'd eagle.　(*Cym.*, 3. 3. 17)

The Titans away, peace reigned in this innocent Paradise. In a country haven the lost daughter of Leontes tended her flowers. "A mistress to most that teach" (4. 4. 593), Perdita planted a garden unlike Hamlet's. Bare of Hamlet's "weeds", it was as free of the "bastard" flowers whose loveliness recalled to her—not beauty's honest plainness, but women's painted lips (4. 4. 101; cf. *Ham.*, 3. 1. 148). But—

Reverend sirs,
For you there's rosemary and rue; these keep
Seeming and savour all the winter long.
　　　　　　　　　　　　　(4. 4. 73)

At a shepherds' "feast" that Timon must have scoffed at, Perdita offered her guests her unspoilt flowers; and, dreaming of yet more, wished still for "flowers o' the spring" to strew her "sweet friend o'er".

O Proserpina,
For the flowers now, that frighted thou let'st fall
From Dis's waggon! . . . (4. 4. 112)

CHAPTER V

THE LAST QUESTION

In his endeavour to cure the evil of the world, Shakespeare has introduced into these dramas, like the Statesman of his earlier plays, Powers divine and human of a kind to ensure at last to men the rational perfection proper and 'natural' to them. The best of earthly Statesmen may fail of his purposes; but the purposes of Heaven, and of the "mortal officers" (*Per.*, 5. 3. 63) Its will inspires, are not to be finally thwarted. Not the "flies of every wind that blows" (*W.T.*, 4. 4. 551), men "cannot but obey the powers above" (*Per.*, 3. 3. 9); allied with fortune's grace "the heavens still must work" (*Cym.*, 4. 3. 41–46; *W.T.*, 3. 2. 29; 5. 1. 36); and, dooming evil, give inevitable promise of a world where men may sing—

> The fingers of the powers above do tune
> The harmony of this peace. (*Cym.*, 5. 5. 466)

Things as "monstrous to our human reason" (*W.T.*, 5. 1. 41) as the resurrection of a dead Thaisa and Hermione (*Per.*, 5. 3; *W.T.*, 5. 3) may attend the supernatural activities of Providence. Men must therefore "awake their faith" (*W.T.*, 5. 3. 95; cf. *Ham.*, 1. 5. 166); and, leaving it to unbelieving Spirits to accuse the Thunderer of human evils no less "monstrous" (*Cym.*, 5. 4. 30–92), accept at last with them (5. 4. 119) the mysterious word of Heaven:

> Be not with mortal accidents opprest:
> No care of yours it is; you know 'tis ours.
> (*Cym.*, 5. 4. 99)

Shakespeare has thus presented a world which, freed from human tragedy, must find, through Heaven's directing power, the ultimate felicity Heaven destines for it. With the wisdom of the Prophet of Israel his thought could now conceive a coming world of men that, rationally conscious of the Power that rules them, "shall be full of the knowledge of the Lord, as the waters cover the sea" (Isaiah, xi. 9).

Yet the reason of the philosopher is not easily satisfied; and the best of answers may provoke at times the worst of questions. Content with his new world, Shakespeare could still continue to question it. Heaven might purpose the ultimate cure of the world's evil; but why Its Providence had admitted an evil to cure remained still a riddle to wonder at. In dooming evil, Heaven would seem to have rejected it as surely as Timon; and that It has for a while accepted it would appear to be one "of those mysteries which heaven will not have earth to know" (*Cor.*, 4. 2. 35). Necessity however is the mother of invention; and in

THE TEMPEST

Shakespeare proceeded, through his study of this question, to complete, with his Theology, his Philosophy of the real nature of man's mysterious universe.

In this play appears a Man who, armed like Oberon with heavenly powers (5. 1. 33–50), lorded it in an Island of which he had dispossessed a crooked monster "capable of all ill" (1. 2. 353). "Got by the devil himself" (1. 2. 319; 4. 1. 188); untamable; uneducable; railing like Sin itself at the Master who controlled him (1. 2. 321); Caliban was to hear a tempest that, roused by the Power of Destiny, bore to his Island three human "devils" no less inhuman than himself (3. 3. 36).

Ariel   You are three men of sin, whom Destiny,—

That hath to instrument this lower world
And what is in't,—the never-surfeited sea
Hath caused to belch up you; and on this island,
Where man doth not inhabit,—you 'mongst men
Being most unfit to live. (3. 3. 53)

Through his magical minister Ariel, Prospero was to bring these sinners forcibly before his Seat of Judgement.

Pros.   My high charms work,
And these mine enemies are all knit up
In their distractions: they now are in my power.
                                        (3. 3. 88)

Prospero however, was not to bring these distracting "fits" on his enemies without suffering some distraction himself. Recalling the "foul play" of a treacherous brother and a heartless king, Prospero recalled a wickedness apt to rouse in him an indignation as acute as Timon's (1. 2. 66–151); and, with omniscient ears discovering presently a new devilry in Caliban, his thought grew darker.

Cal.   'Tis a custom with him
I' th' afternoon to sleep: there thou mayst brain him,
Having first seized his books; or with a log
Batter his skull, or paunch him with a stake,
Or cut his wezand with thy knife. (3. 2. 95)

At the hour of Caliban's wicked attempt (4. 1. 139) Timon and Hamlet spoke their word in Prospero. In a "passion" that worked him "strongly" (4. 1. 143), Prospero "fanged" the world of man and threatened to reduce it, like a ghostly pageant, to an insubstantial "congregation of vapours". The world might tremble for a moment lest his "so potent art" (5. 1. 33) should end it:

Pros.   The cloud-capp'd towers, the gorgeous palaces,

181

> The solemn temples, the great globe itself,
> Yea, all which it inherit, shall dissolve,
> And, like this insubstantial pageant faded,
> Leave not a rack behind. We are such stuff
> As dreams are made on; and our little life
> Is rounded with a sleep. (4. 1. 152)

Man must, however, accept a world that Heaven Itself has accepted; and the Providence ruling in Prospero soon stilled his "beating mind" (4. 1. 163). Unnaturally touched "with anger so distemper'd" (4. 1. 145), he resumed Heaven's purpose in him so to order his world's happenings that "not so much perdition as an hair" (1. 2. 30) should trouble his enemies.

Pros.	Now does my project gather to a head . . .
	Say, my spirit,
	How fares the king and's followers? . . .
Ari.	The king,
	His brother, and yours, abide all three distracted . . .
	Your charm so strongly works 'em,
	That if you now beheld them, your affections
	Would become tender.
Pros.	And mine shall.

> Hast thou, which art but air, a touch, a feeling
> Of their afflictions, and shall not myself,
> One of their kind, that relish all as sharply,
> Passion as they, be kindlier moved than thou art?
> Though with their high wrongs I am struck to the
> quick,
> Yet with my nobler reason 'gainst my fury
> Do I take part: the rarer action is
> In virtue than in vengeance: they being penitent,
> The sole drift of my purpose doth extend
> Not a frown further. (5. 1. 1; 3. 3. 81)

Prospero's "rough magic" (5. 1. 33–50) had left men in the

chains of Heaven's just Power. A closing magic that displaced it (5. 1. 50–51) was to leave them in the arms of Heaven's Mercy. Justice turned her head away, Prospero smiled at Timon, and, accepting the "demi-devils" of the earth, embraced and, embracing, forgave them:—to an ignoble Alonso, "I embrace thy body" (5. 1. 109); to a worse, and colder brother, "unnatural though thou art" (5. 1. 74–79), "I do forgive thy rankest fault,—all of them" (5. 1. 131).

Welcome, my friends all! (5. 1. 125)

Caliban the untamable was himself in the end to petition repentantly for the grace of his Master.

> Pros.   Go, sirrah, to my cell . . .
>   as you look
>   To have my pardon, trim it handsomely.
> Cal.   Ay, that I will; and I'll be wise hereafter,
>   And seek for grace. (5. 1. 291)

With his acceptance of the world Prospero has answered Timon, as in *Measure for Measure* the Duke had answered Hamlet. Ministers of Heaven, each had shone like Heaven on Heaven's children; rather their Lover than their Judge, each had made his "sun to rise on the good and on the evil", and sent his "rain on the just and on the unjust".

Accepted by Heaven, yet man's evil is still doomed by Heaven; and without some purpose of its own its passing existence in men must remain a wonder to marvel at. In the three plays preceding *The Tempest* Shakespeare had treated of the salvation of man; but in *Cymbeline* he had divined, in Heaven's punishment of evil, a peculiar reason for Heaven's acceptance of it. In a stormy vision a sinful Posthumus (*Cym.*, 5. 4. 63) had listened in wonder to the mysterious word of a God:

'Whom best I love, I cross: to make my gift,
The more delay'd, delighted.'
                                    (*Cym.*, 5. 4. 101–108)

As boldly Shakespeare was to conceive, in the present storm
of *The Tempest*, of a heavenly Prospero as pouring his crosses
on men that their delay might make his gifts the more prized
by them.

Heaven must Itself appear of more worth to a man who has
had to win his way to It; and the loveliest of things be prized
the more if Heaven withhold them for a while from him
(*M. for M.*, 4. 3. 113). Prospero was to "cross", with his
own daughter, her true lover, and by their crosses crown
them.

Pros.   They are both in either's powers: but this swift
                                    business
         I must uneasy make, lest too light winning
         Make the prize light. (1. 2. 450–485)

Very "uneasily" Ferdinand was to cry out, with his mistress,
against the irrational sternness of Prospero:

            I must remove
         Some thousands of these logs, and pile them up,
         Upon a sore injunction: my sweet mistress
         Weeps when she sees me work, and says, such
                                    baseness
         Had never like executor. (3. 1. 9)

Betrothed at last to one another, Miranda and Ferdinand were
not to enjoy each other instantly; but, still "delay'd", to make
the father's gift the more "delighted" (4. 1. 13).

Heaven's seeming severity was visited through the "crabbed"
Prospero (3. 1. 8), as well as on his innocent daughter and her
lover, on an innocent old man honoured by him as "the good
old lord Gonzalo".

Ari.   His tears run down his beard, like winter's drops
           From eaves of reeds. (5. 1. 15)

Human innocence may win through suffering a joy else wanted by it, but human evil must receive blows as severe as Lear's before Heaven offers Its gifts to its repentance. On the guiltless Gonzalo's evil companions the crosses of Prospero's justice fell like hail:

Ari.   The king,
          His brother, and yours, abide all three distracted,
          And the remainder mourning over them,
          Brimful of sorrow and dismay. (5. 1. 11)

As fearful crosses were to fall on others among them who, with Caliban, had made men's lusts their pleasure.

Pros.   I will plague them all,
          Even to roaring. . . .
Ari.   Hark, they roar!
Pros.   Let them be hunted soundly. (4. 1. 192)

Prospero's severities however hid, like Heaven's, a smile in them.

              To the brightest beams
          Distracted clouds give way.
                      (*All's Well*, 5. 3. 34)

"Calm seas, auspicious gales" (5. 1. 314) were to follow the Tempest of Prospero. Men who had lost "themselves" were now to find their loss their profit (5. 1. 212; cf. *A. and C.*, 2. 1. 5–8); and rejoicing beyond "a common joy" to divine at last the secret purpose of Heaven's mysterious "crosses" (5. 1. 199–215; *Cym.*, 5. 4. 99–102).

Such, it seems, was Shakespeare's solution of the perplexing "problem of evil". It is for man's ultimate benefit that

Heaven has admitted evil into the world. In making "uneasy" man's attainment of his rational nature evil is destined to rein-force and invigorate it. The enjoyment of its prizes without a painful "winning" of them is not for man his perfect enjoy-ment. In missing the painful crosses of the Father the sinless Elder Son of the parable missed the best gift of the Father.

> For it so falls out,
> That what we have we prize not to the worth
> Whiles we enjoy it, but being lack'd and lost,
> Why then we rack the value, then we find
> The virtue that possession would not show us
> Whiles it was ours. (*Much Ado*, 4. 1. 216)

Doomed finally to perish, yet evil must for a while have its heavenly part to play in the world; and a world of sinless perfection must be one possessed of no more than a "common joy".

Man must thus view the world with other than the eyes of a Timon. Evil as it may be, the world cannot be a Medusa to turn man's heart to stone. Men may blanch at the sight of it, but to the foreseeing Prophet evil is the promise of Heaven's best of gifts to Its children:

> "Bring forth quickly the best robe, and put it on
> him . . . For this my son was dead, and is alive
> again; he was lost, and is found . . ."

Being "aware of himself, and of God, and of Things", by a "certain eternal necessity", Shakespeare could acquire, like Spinoza, a "true acquiescence of his spirit". Why evil had entered the world appeared as intelligible as that Heaven had accepted its presence there. The poet crowned his philosophy with a thought that had once calmed a tempest in himself:

O benefit of ill! now I find true

186

That better is by evil still made better;
And ruin'd love, when it is built anew,
Grows fairer than at first, more strong, far greater.
  So I return rebuked to my content,
  And gain by ill thrice more than I have spent.
                                        (*Son.* 119)

INDEX

189